GOD DOES HIS BEST WORK AT NIGHT

John 8·12

TOMMY COMBS

HCombs

Published by

LIFEBRIDGE
B O O K S
P.O. BOX 49428
CHARLOTTE, NC 28277

Printed in the United States of America.

DEDICATION

To my precious wife, Linda—
the best gift God ever gave me.
To my son, Matthew—a Prince with God.
To my daughter, Sara Elizabeth
—God's Princess.

ACKNOWLEDGMENTS

To a very special group of people whose
dedication to God I greatly respect:

Pastor Claude Moore, Dr. Oral Roberts,
Evangelist Perry Stone, Prophet M. H. Kennedy,
and my spiritual father, Dr. T. L. Lowery.

CONTENTS

INTRODUCTION

I don't know what you are going through at this very moment—but God does. This one thing is sure; the Lord has inspired me to write this book for a special purpose, and I believe it is because He knows you need these words today.

No matter how difficult the circumstances or how black the situation seems to be, I can tell you from personal experience and on the authority of God's Word that there is light from above waiting to shine on you.

My friend, there is no reason to fear the night. Why can I say this? Because in the darkest hour the Master breaks through and performs His greatest miracles.

When the skies turn dark and the situation seems beyond your ability to control, this is when the Almighty arrives to intervene on your behalf—to do for you what you are incapable of doing for yourself.

The most severe trial of your life may arrive when you least expect it—and you may be in a place where you think God has forgotten and forsaken you.

Don't despair! You are about to discover that as a child of God, He has a perfect plan for you and you are on His timetable. In fact, the Lord is preparing a place for you where night will be completely eliminated!

I want to introduce you to God's Son—the Light of the World. When you have a divine encounter with Him, your darkness will end forever!

Get ready for your spirits to be lifted and filled with hope and expectation. Yes, God does His best work at night!

– Tommy Combs

CHAPTER 1

OUT OF THE DARKNESS

Who is among you that feareth the Lord,
that obeyeth the voice of his servant, that walketh
in darkness, and hath no light? Let him trust in the
name of the Lord, and stay upon his God.
— ISAIAH 50:10

With all of my heart, I believe the Lord has placed this book into your hand at this very moment to accomplish a divine purpose in your life.

I don't know the circumstances you are going through—whether it be physical, financial, or relational —but God does. And what you are about to discover holds the key to your deliverance. It is a principle you can apply again and again, regardless of the situation you face.

Let's start at the beginning. We know that God created the heaven and the earth. *"And the earth was without form, and void; and darkness was upon the face of the deep. And the Spirit of God moved upon the face of the waters. And God said, Let there be light: and there was light. And God saw the light, that it was good: and God divided the light from the darkness. And God called the light Day, and the darkness he called Night. And the evening and the morning were the first day"* (Genesis 1:2-5).

Most of us read this passage and fail to truly recognize what happened. The Bible tells us that on the first day, in the midst of darkness He created light—and then He divided the dark (evening) and light (day).

Each morning we arise, go to work, school, or whatever. Then we come home, eat supper, watch television, do our homework and get ready for bed (and hopefully read our Bible and pray sometime in between).

Our activities are primarily in the daytime, but God includes what will happen in the nighttime hours. The Bible says the evening (night) and the day make the first day. This means night came first—then the day.

You see, the Lord views things different from you and me—His thoughts are not our thoughts, His ways are not our ways (Isaiah 55:8-9).

Creation was God's greatest work: and it took place at night.

YOUR STEPS ARE ORDERED

If you thought the moment you were saved that all your troubles and trials would be over and never return, I have news for you. Without adversities, there would be no need for a higher power in your life! The reason God allows troubles and trials is because it places us in a position to be dependent and call on Him.

If everything went the way we always wanted it to, we wouldn't need God. But He created an answer (Jesus) so that we could survive any adversity.

> *The reason God allows troubles and trials is because it places us in a position to be dependent and call on Him.*

As a believer, the Lord is watching your walk and guiding your path. David writes, *"The steps of a good man are ordered by the Lord: and he delighteth in his way. Though he fall, he shall not be utterly cast down: for the Lord upholdeth him with his hand"* (Psalm 37:23-24).

You complain to yourself, "Why am I going through this? Why is this happening to my family or my church? Why?"

It's because this is what God has on the menu for your life. There are seasons and times when things are good or bad, but be assured, the Almighty is still in

11

control. He will never abandon you.

GOD KNOWS YOU

Perhaps you believe like the people in Isaiah's day, *"The Lord hath forsaken me, and my Lord hath forgotten me"* (Isaiah 49:14).

> **It is essential to remember that God knew and saw you before you were ever born.**

But listen to what God is saying: *"Can a women forget her sucking child, that she should not have compassion on the son of her womb? Yea, they may forget yet will I not forget thee. Behold, I have graven thee upon the palms of my hands; thy walls are continually before me"* (verses 15-16).

It is essential to remember that God knew and saw you before you were ever born. The Bible tells us, *"Before I formed thee in the belly I knew thee; and before thou camest forth out of the womb I sanctified thee, and I ordained thee a prophet unto the nations"* (Jeremiah 1:5).

Your heavenly Father has a picture of you, placed it in His palm and declared, "I will not forget you, My child!"

He is constantly watching. So if you feel the darkness

of night has fallen and there is no hope, remember: *"Who is among you that feareth the Lord, that obeyeth the voice of his servant, that walketh in darkness, and hath no light? Let him trust in the name of the Lord, and stay upon his God"* (Isaiah 50.10).

THE PROCESS OF DEVELOPMENT

Before an artist can paint a picture, he has to have the image engraved in his mind. He must visualize it before he can transfer it onto the canvas.

Let's look at the process. When you get ready for a professional picture to be taken, you put on your best clothes, comb your hair, brush your teeth, and make sure everything is as perfect as it can be. You may even turn a certain way to hide your double chin or crooked nose. Then you stand still, smile, and say "cheese."

After the photo shoot, you don't immediately jump up and show the finished product to everyone. If the photographer uses film, he takes it to the darkroom for processing.

As Christians, we sometimes find ourselves in dark situations and don't understand what is taking place. But there is a divine purpose and a plan. This is where the negatives—those things which will not benefit us—are stripped away. We may not always like the process, but it is the method God uses.

There are times we attempt to hold onto those hindrances the Lord wants to remove from the picture. I'm referring to negative thoughts, talk, habits, and negative relationships.

Where does God do His best work? In the dark place.

In is only in God's developing room that He builds character and trust.

Now you are ready for the developing stage. And this is a process which takes time. All of a sudden, God begins to shape and mold you. You don't sing one song in the church choir and decide to record an album. Neither do you preach just one sermon and decide to go on the evangelistic trail.

It is only in God's developing room that He builds character and trust. What you are in public is a direct result of what God makes you in private!

DON'T TOUCH THE PICTURE!

Yes, there are going to be ominous times when dark clouds roll in, blocking the light. But this is when you must stand firm and place your faith in the Lord. Christians who continually complain and whine have forgotten who they are! Never forget that you are blessed coming in and blessed going out. You are the head and not the tail. You are a child of the King and an heir to God's throne.

Most important, you have a right to be what the Lord has called you to be. In the developing process, the picture of your life becomes clearer and the Lord's purpose comes into sharp focus.

God is the ultimate photographer, but if we make the wrong moves, we can damage the process. For example, we can harm a picture in the darkroom by just touching it. This is why we can't place our hands on what the Lord is doing.

LET GOD FINISH THE WORK

Do you remember what happened to Abraham? The Lord spoke to him in a dark place! As he was sleeping, God told him that his seed would be a mighty nation, so many in number that the people couldn't be counted—like stars in the sky, or sands on the shore.

Abraham awoke, acted on God's directive and followed His promise. But it wasn't long until Abraham began to interfere in God's picture. He complained, "It's not happening soon enough. My wife, Sarah, is barren. We still don't have a son."

As a result, he entered a dark room with Sarah's

handmaiden Hagar and produced Ishmael—that which God had not planned for him to produce!

Abraham made the mistake of tampering with what God was trying to accomplish. The lesson is that you can't fix a situation God is not yet finished with.

> *Into every life comes a dark season where you have to let the Lord accomplish His work.*

Instead of using a closet of prayer, some choose a course of deceit. We think we can repair every problem, but the situation may call for fervent prayer, fasting, and crying out to God, "Lord, I can't handle this alone. You have to take control."

Then tell Him, "I know there is a reason I am in this dark place, but I give my life to You. Remove the negatives and develop me to my full destiny!"

Into every life comes a dark season where you have to let the Lord accomplish His work.

WHILE ADAM SLEPT

After God created the earth—including the first man—He said to Adam, "I am going to put you to sleep."

Since he and the Creator talked together every day, I can imagine Adam asking, "Why? What is the reason?"

The Lord responds, "I am going to put you in a state

where you are not going to know what I am doing."

Adam likely replied, "But Lord, I want to help You. I want to be a part of this."

God was insistent, "No. I've got to do this without your help, but when you wake up, everything is going to be all right."

As scripture records, *"And the Lord God caused a deep sleep to fall upon Adam, and he slept: and he took one of his ribs, and closed up the flesh instead thereof; And the rib, which the Lord God had taken from man, made he a woman, and brought her unto the man"* (Genesis 2:21-22).

The next morning, Adam woke up and was in for quite a surprise. During the night, God made Eve!

Adam probably looked over at her and exclaimed, "Wow!"

All of a sudden he was happy and filled with joy. Why? Because God does His best work at night.

What do you think Adam's response would be the next time God told him, "I'm going to put you to sleep"?

Would he argue or ask to help? No, I can hear him agreeing, "Go for it God! You do the work. I'm ready!"

When the Almighty places you in the dark, He is just preparing you for a daytime experience. The Bible tells us that *"weeping may endure for a night, but joy cometh in the morning"* (Psalm 30:5).

You must have faith and trust before the manifestation becomes a reality. Faith says, "I expect God to take care of this situation." Trust says, "I will stand here and believe until God answers."

"LET ME PLOW THE WAY"

Far too often, Christians tell the Lord, "It's okay. I can handle this."

I've heard about couples who get married after their first date. Excited, they exclaim, "This is the one!" Then, before the ink dries on the marriage license, they file for divorce!

When you ask them what happened, they respond, "Well, we really didn't know what we were getting into."

Remember, it is always better to want something you don't have than to have something you don't want!

If you are unhappy being single, be patient. Stay in that state until God gives you a mate—and don't hurry the process. If you don't like being an associate pastor, remain faithful until the Lord tells you to move forward.

Years ago, when I started to speak at churches and conventions, I thought I had to do all the work myself: send letters, call the right people in the right places, prepare great messages, and do what was politically correct. But God told me, "Let Me plow the way. Allow

Me to open the doors."

So I gave up on my human efforts and let God take control. As a result I've traveled to more places and seen more miracles than I could have ever imagined. Why? Because I let the Lord take charge!

STOP AND LISTEN

In the darkness, our imagination works overtime and we often see things that aren't really there. In truth, however, there may be no emergency, no danger. As one person told me, "It was so pitch black that I thought someone was coming after me. All I needed was the light to show the way."

> *In the darkness, our imagination works overtime and we often see things that aren't really there.*

When you can't see what tomorrow holds, don't make hasty decisions. Rather, be still and let God be God. When you find yourself in a dark place, all you need to do is stand and see the salvation of the Lord.

Far too many are frightened by the night and cry out, "Lord, what do I do now? Who do I call? Do I pray eight hours and fast for two days?

Stop and listen to what the Lord is telling you. Stay where you are and He will show you the way out.

The same God who called you, equips, ordains, and anoints you. Stand still and let the Lord take care of the situation. Everything is going to be all right! He will bring you what you need if you will allow Him to do the work.

GET READY FOR THE RAIN

The Bible tells of a wise man who built his house on solid rock and a foolish man who built his on shifting sand. However, when it began to rain, it just didn't fall on the foolish, it also descended on the wise.

The wise man knew something about troubles and trials. He said, "I knew where to build so my foundation would stand the test."

Yes, it gets dark and stormy, but when circumstances are beyond your ability, that's when God steps in and does what you can't do for yourself.

When the nights are the darkest, listen to the Lord, who is saying, "Let Me take care of you! Trust Me, I will never leave you or forsake you."

CHAPTER 2

"COME FORTH"

Our friend Lazarus sleepth; but I go, that
I may awake him out of sleep.

– JOHN 11:11

In the town of Bethany, about two miles from Jerusalem, a man named Lazarus was very sick.

This was the village where Mary and her sister, Martha, lived—the same Mary who anointed the Lord's feet with ointment and then wiped them dry with her hair (Luke 7:44-45).

It was their brother, Lazarus, who was ill. This family was close to Jesus and that is why the sisters sent word to Him, *"Lord, behold, he whom thou lovest is sick"* (John 11:3).

Upon receiving the message, Jesus said, *"This sickness is not unto death, but for the glory of God, that the Son of God might be glorified thereby"* (verse 4).

The Lord obviously knew the miracle which was

about to take place. Jesus was so confident that He stayed beyond Jordan two more days before deciding to travel to Bethany.

The disciples were concerned, warning Him, *"Master, the Jews of late sought to stone thee; and goest thou thither again?"* (verse 8).

Jesus, however, was determined to make the journey. He told the disciples, *"Our friend Lazarus sleepth; but I go, that I may awake him out of sleep"* (verse 11).

The disciples thought Lazarus was just taking a nap and that he would wake up feeling fine. But Jesus was talking about actual death. In fact, He said to them plainly, *"Lazarus is dead"* (verse 14). And the Lord explained that He was glad for their sakes that He wasn't there—because they were about to be given new evidence for believing. So Jesus and His disciples went to Bethany.

THE RESURRECTION AND THE LIFE

When Jesus finally arrived, Lazarus had already been dead for four days. Many Jewish friends of the family were present, mourning with Mary and Martha over the loss of their brother.

Scripture records that Martha heard Jesus was approaching and went out on the road to meet Him, while

Mary stayed at the house.

The first words Martha uttered to Jesus were: *"Lord, if thou hadst been here, my brother had not died"* (verse 21). Then, with great faith, she added, *"But I know, that even now, whatsoever thou wilt ask of God, God will give it thee"* (verse 22).

At that moment, with divine authority, Jesus made this bold statement: *"Your brother shall rise again"* (verse 23).

> **With divine authority, Jesus made this bold statement: "Your brother shall rise again."**

Martha, who thought Jesus was referring to some future event, responded, *"I know that he shall rise again in the resurrection at the last day"* (verse 24).

But the Lord was speaking of the here and now. He looked at her and said, *"I am the resurrection and the life: he that believeth in me, though he were dead, yet shall he live. And whosoever liveth and believeth in me shall never die"* (verses 25-26).

Then He asked Martha, "Do you believe this?"

Martha responded that she did. *"I believe that thou art the Christ, the Son of God, which should come into the world"* (verse 27).

TEARS OF THE SAVIOR

Martha ran back to the house and quietly told Mary that Jesus had arrived and would like to speak with her. So she quickly went to the place just outside of Bethany where the Lord had first spoken to Martha.

When the Jewish friends, who had been sympathizing with her, saw Mary run from the house, they followed. They thought she was going to the tomb to weep.

But Mary came to the place where Jesus was waiting and fell at His feet, crying—and repeating the same words as Martha—*"Lord, if thou hadst been here, my brother had not died"* (verse 32).

Witnessing Mary and her friends weeping, the spirit of Jesus was troubled. He inquired, *"Where have ye laid him?"* (verse 33).

They asked Jesus to follow them to the grave.

At that point, we find the shortest verse recorded in scripture, but it conveys the depth of Christ's love. The Bible tells us, *"Jesus wept"* (verse 35).

Some of the Jews who were there commented on how much Jesus loved Lazarus. But others were critical: *"Could not this man, which opened the eyes of the blind, have caused that even this man should not have died?"* (verse 37).

AN AMAZING SCENE

Still deeply troubled, Jesus arrived at the tomb.

It was a simple cave in the side of a hill with a stone laid against it. The Lord commanded, *"Take ye away the stone"* (verse 39).

Martha tried to explain that her brother had been dead for four days and the stench would be unbearable. But Jesus looked her in the eyes and asked, *"Said I not unto thee, that, if thou wouldest believe, thou shouldest see the glory of God?"* (verse 40).

At the Lord's direction, they rolled the stone away from the tomb. Then Jesus looked up to heaven and said, *"Father, I thank thee that thou hast heard me. And I knew that thou hearest me always: but because of the people which stand by I said it, that they may believe that thou hast sent me"* (verses 41-42).

> **At the Lord's direction, they rolled the stone away from the tomb.**

The Bible records that when Jesus had spoken those words, He cried with a loud voice, *"Lazarus, come forth"* (verse 43).

At that moment, Lazarus, bound hand and foot with graveclothes, and his face covered with a cloth, came forth out of the tomb!

To the amazed onlookers, Jesus instructed, *"Loose him, and let him go"* (verse 44).

GOD IN THREE FORMS

I love this story, because every time I read of the miracle of Lazarus, I learn much more about the Lord. Jesus deeply *loved* this man—there was a bond between them. It is evident in John's account that he is concerned over our concept of Christ, and how we think about the Lord. John wants us to know that Christianity is not a religion of rules, but one of relationship.

> *Christianity is not a religion of rules, but one of relationship.*

In order for us to walk as our heavenly Father intends, we must know Jesus for ourselves. In fact, John presents God to us in three distinct forms:

First: The written Word—Logos

John begins his Gospel with these words: *"In the beginning was the Word, and the Word was with God, and the Word was God"* (John 1:1).

We know that God is a Spirit, but the Almighty wanted us to understand His thoughts—so He transformed them into written words (*logos*) so that you and I can better know Him.

Second: The Incarnate Word—Jesus in the flesh

Scripture declares, *"The Word was made flesh, and dwelt among us"* (John 1:14).

The thoughts of God came into our world in a "canopy of flesh." As a result we can behold the only begotten Son of God. This was a voluntary act of the Almighty. The *logos* (thought) of God became flesh because He wanted to reveal Himself.

Jesus was sent to earth and dwelt among us so that you and I (mankind) could behold Him. As long as He remained a thought, we could not see God, but when He became flesh, we could see Him and enjoy a personal relationship.

Because of this, the Incarnate Jesus becomes "Shekinah Glory" in open manifestation.

Third: The spoken Word—Rhema

This is the sword (Word) of the spirit Jesus spoke of when He proclaimed, *"The words [rhema] that I speak unto you, they are spirit, and they are life"* (John 6:63).

Today, the revealed Word of God is spoken to your spirit.

THROUGH THE WORD

John, the forerunner of Jesus, possessed all three: (1) he had the *logos* Word—the written Torah of Moses, (2) the *Incarnate* Word—his close association with Jesus, and (3) the *rhema* Word—the Spirit-revealed, spoken Word of God.

The Bible is the expression of Christ to us, who is the image of God. So, if I want to experience Jesus, I must know the Word:

- **In the Word is your Salvation**
- **In the Word is your Healing**
- **In the Word is your Peace**
- **In the Word is your Joy**
- **In the Word is your Strength**
- **In the Word are your Blessings**

In your dark time—when you can't see a solution and feel all alone, that no one cares or understands—you have the Word of God. And through the Word, Jesus is *"whatever"* you need.

WHAT IS YOUR SITUATION?

In the village of Bethany, where Lazarus was already placed in a tomb, Jesus—the Logos, the Incarnate, and the Rhema—walked up to Mary and said, "I am here to reveal Myself."

This is important: There must be a sickness before healing is revealed. There must be a death before life is revealed.

At the tomb of Lazarus, everybody was about to know who Jesus really is. He created (allowed) a situation so He could be made manifest.

There must be a sickness before healing is revealed. There must be a death before life is revealed.

This has been true of God the Father, God the Son, and God the Holy Spirit throughout scripture:

- He created a situation and He called it Jehovah Nissi—The Lord is my banner.

- He created a situation and He called it Jehovah Jireh—The Lord is my provider.

- He created a situation and He called it Jehovah Shalom— The Lord is my peace.

- He created a situation and He called it Jehovah Tsidkenu—The Lord is my righteousness.

- He created a situation and He called it Jehovah Rohi—The Lord is my shepherd.

- He created a situation and He called it Jehovah Shammah—The Lord is ever present.

- He created a situation and He called it Jehovah Rophe—The Lord is my healer.

Whatever circumstance you are in at this present moment has come your way for only one reason. It is so Jesus can be revealed.

GOD'S TIMETABLE

Mary and Martha were impatient and in a hurry for the Lord to move on behalf of their brother, and today we react the same way.

Have you ever felt like the Lord wasn't responding fast enough for you? You pay your tithes, teach Sunday School, help the needy and lead a righteous life. Shouldn't Jesus be quick to answer?

One person complained to the Lord, "I go to church every time the doors are open, yet I'm sick, broke, and have no end of problems. Why me? I can think of a hundred people in this church who don't do half as much, and they seem to be getting along just fine. Help me, Lord. I am Your friend. I'm serving You everyday! Do

You understand me?"

This is the way Mary and Martha were thinking. If anyone should have been able to get Jesus to their house to pray for their brother, it was these two women.

Jesus was preparing them for a miracle—and He was about to receive glory!

But in the Lord's plan, the situation regarding Lazarus was *"for the glory of God, that the Son of God might be glorified thereby"* (John 11:4). In other words, Jesus was preparing them for a miracle—and He was about to receive glory!

The Lord has His own timetable.

THE TESTING OF OUR FAITH

Do you really know your Savior? This is essential because the Son of God will use those He is well acquainted with. Why? Because when your answer arrives, you will tell everyone you meet about your saving, healing, and delivering friend—Jesus.

In Bethany, while the Lord was in the process of revealing who He truly was, the faith of Mary and Martha was being severely tested. You see, sickness, grief, death, and other problems play havoc with your faith.

31

So while Jesus is relaxed because He knows He is going to receive glory, you and I are worrying and crying. But remember, it's just a prelude for the Lord to reveal Himself—even if some things in our life need to die.

Finally, at the tomb:

- It didn't matter that Lazarus had been dead for days.
- It didn't matter that his heart had stopped.
- It didn't matter that his blood was no longer circulating.
- It didn't matter that the body was decomposing.

Jesus only needed to say three words before the situation was totally transformed. He declared, "Lazarus, come forth!"—and what was dead suddenly sprung back to life.

SPEAK TO YOUR CIRCUMSTANCES

As a child of the Son of God, and because Christ is living in you, at this very moment you can declare deliverance to your circumstances:

- **Joy...Come Forth!**

- **Peace...Come Forth!**

- **Finances...Come Forth!**

- **Healing...Come Forth!**

- **Marriage...Come Forth!**

- **Victory...Come Forth!**

Speak the Word over your situation. Now is your time.

CHAPTER 3

FOUR DOORS OUT OF DARKNESS

I have set before thee an open door,
and no man can shut it.
— REVELATION 3:8

The number four is significant in scripture. It represents God's control over the world He created:

- We have four seasons—summer, autumn, winter, and spring.

- There are four divisions of the day—morning, noon, evening, and midnight.

- God provided four major provisions for man—earth, air, fire, and water.

- There are four directions on earth—north, south, east, and west.

In the New Testament we find there are four categories of unclean spirits you and I must battle: *"For we wrestle not against flesh and blood, but [1] against principalities, [2] against powers, [3] against the rulers of the darkness of this world, [4] against spiritual wickedness in high places"* (Ephesians 6:12).

These four levels of demonic powers attempt to block us from God—to ruin our relationship with Him and place us in the path of temptation, oppression, and depression.

Thankfully, we have a power to help us that is far greater than the enemy.

Thankfully, we have a power to help us that is far greater than the enemy.

Back in the days of King Nebuchadnezzar, there were three Hebrew children, Shadrach, Meshach, and Abednego, who refused to bow down to the golden idol the king had set up. Because of their disobedience they were thrown into a fiery furnace. But when the king looked down to see their demise, he was in for quite a shock. He asked, *"Did not we cast three men bound into the midst of the fire? They answered and said unto the king, True, O king. He answered and said, Lo, I see four men loose, walking in the midst of the fire, and they have no hurt; and the form of the fourth is like the Son of God"* (Daniel 3:24-25).

The fourth Man! Jesus!

FOUR SQUADS OF SOLDIERS

Let me share another story where four significant events occurred. After the Day of Pentecost, when the message of Christ began to be preached and the early church was growing rapidly, King Herod decided to go after some of the early Christian leaders. He murdered, James, the brother of John. Then, when Herod saw how his own popularity was soaring with the Jewish leaders, he had Peter arrested and thrown in jail during Passover Week.

Herod had every intention of lynching this disciple as soon as the festivities were over.

The Bible tells us that Peter was delivered to *"four quaternions of soldiers...intending after Easter to bring him forth to the people"* (Acts 12:4).

A quaternion consists of four squads of four soldiers each. During the four watches, two were chained to Peter, and two were standing guard. These were not just a band of untrained, ragamuffin men, these were Herod's elite.

However, something else was taking place on Peter's

behalf. Scripture records that when the believers in Jerusalem heard he was a prisoner, *"Prayer was made without ceasing of the church unto God for him"* (verse 5).

What took place next is nothing less than a miracle from the hand of God. As we look closely at the story, we see Four Doors out of Darkness—that are significant for you and me today.

Door Number One:
The Door Inside You

Just a few hours before Herod planned to have him killed, the Bible gives this account: *"The same night Peter was sleeping between two soldiers, bound with two chains: and the keepers before the door kept the prison"* (Acts 12:6).

It was at night—when God does His best work!

The very first door that Peter had to go through on his way to freedom and deliverance was called the "inner ward." It was the deepest and darkest part of the prison and represents the door that is inside of you!

This is the private, secret area of your life that is hidden in a dark place no one knows except you personally. In this inner sanctum you wrestle and struggle with issues that weigh upon your very soul. It could be the burden of illness, finances, a family matter, or a battle with an addiction or habit that is ruining your very existence.

This is the chamber that satan always targets for attack. Perhaps it is a problem in your marriage. You seem to have everything worked out, love is flourishing again and then, wham! The devil hits once more.

Others may be trapped by mental or physical abuse that happened in the past—a secret known only to God. But the memory of the tragedy lingers and refuses to go away.

> *Be assured today that the Lord desires to bring you out of that inner ward —the first door.*

Be assured today that the Lord desires to bring you out of that inner ward—the first door. He wants to set you free, and the first step is an anointing He will place upon you that will loose this bondage and give you liberty.

HE WASN'T DREAMING

You may have doubts and question, "How do I escape from this deep, dark place?"

Let's look at how God intervened on Peter's behalf. The Bible records, *"And, behold, the angel of the Lord came upon him, and a light shined in the prison: and he smote Peter on the side, and raised him up, saying, Arise up quickly. And his chains fell off from his hands"* (Acts 12:7).

The angel told him, *"Gird thyself, and bind on thy sandals, And so he did. And he saith unto him, Cast thy garment about thee, and follow me"* (verse 8).

Peter thought he was dreaming—but he followed the angel's orders anyway.

"I'M FREE!"

Like Peter, you can't escape by yourself. It takes a heavenly visitation, a touch from God to open this heavy door. Remember, it is *"Not by might, nor by power, but by my spirit, saith the Lord of hosts"* (Zechariah 4:6).

If you are ever going to walk out of the inner ward and be free from the spirit of fear or thoughts that constantly ensnare you, ask God for a Holy Ghost intervention!

Notice that the angel told Peter, "Arise up quickly." And when he did, the chains fell off.

The Lord is saying the same thing to you: "Get up!"

You don't need to wait until you are free before you respond to God's voice. Do what He asks—and whatever binds you will be loosed.

Decide in your spirit to respond to the Lord. Rise up in your faith, in your confession, and in your praise. Tell satan, "I'm not staying in this mess any longer. I am getting up! I am free!"

Thirty seconds in God's presence will change you forever.

FROM CAPTIVITY TO LIBERTY

Refuse to listen to the lies of satan when he tells you that you will have to suffer with disease or torment the rest of your life—and that you will never be delivered or healed.

Arise! God will turn your captivity into liberty. He will bless you and give you favor, but you must "get up quickly!"

Arise! God will turn your captivity into liberty.

As we learned in the story of Joseph, what the devil meant for evil, God will turn around for your good. Out of the ashes will come newness of life. It is your choice. Start declaring:

- This is the day the Lord has made. I will rejoice and be glad in it (Psalm 118:24).

- He is able to do exceeding abundantly above all I ask or think (Ephesians 3:20).

- I am more than a conquerer through Him who loves me (Romans 8:37).

- Greater is He who is in me than He who is in the world (1 John 4:4).

- I will bless the Lord at all times: His praise shall continually be in my mouth (Psalm 34:1).

When you are free from your own self—your private battles, secret sins, and personal demons, you are ready to move toward the second door.

Door Number Two:
Freedom from the Expectations of People

When Peter realized the miracle which had taken place, he said, *"Now I know of a surety, that the Lord hath sent his angel, and hath delivered me out of the hand of Herod, and from all the expectation of the people of the Jews"* (Acts 12:11).

The moment you become free from what others say about you, door number two swings open.

Many are intimidated by the opinions of those around them. "Did you see that look in her eye?" "I can't believe how he talks about me!"

Friend, once you are liberated on the inside, you must make sure you are free on the outside so people can no longer pull the strings and control your life. Only then can you turn a deaf ear to what others say and declare, "I am free!" No longer will their expectations dominate you.

I no longer focus on the opinions of others. I only care what God thinks!

I have learned to enter into a place in God where I feel safe and secure. I no longer focus on the opinions of others. I only care about what God thinks!

- People didn't die on the cross for me. Jesus did!

- People didn't forgive and save me! Jesus did!

- People will not heal me. Jesus will!

- People will not judge me. Jesus will!

- People didn't set me free. Jesus did!

It's time to stop fearing man and fear the Lord. As the Bible declares, *"The fear of man bringeth a snare"* (Proverbs 28:25), *"but the fear of God is wisdom"* (Job 28:28).

Door Number Three:

The Iron Gate to the City

Peter followed the angel. *"When they were past the first and the second ward, they came unto the iron gate that leadeth unto the city; which opened to them of his own accord: and they went out, and passed on through one street; and forthwith the angel departed from him"* (Acts 12:10).

On the other side of the Iron Gate is the city where you live. It is here you are called to take the Good News to your sons, daughters, friends, and business associates. It is also the place where alcoholics, drug addicts, prostitutes and even former church members live.

When you are free from the expectations of others, this Iron Gate will open.

When you are free from yourself and the expectations of others, this Iron Gate will open. What's even more exciting, it will swing wide on its own accord! God will cause this door to open automatically.

Just take the first step and the Lord will do the rest. You will begin ministering to people you once thought were impossible to reach. God will bring them to you.

When Noah built the ark, the Lord didn't tell Noah to

fill it up with animals. God's instructions were simply to "build it." God led the animals into the ark.

When the Lord unlocks the Iron Gate to your city, the spirit of God will begin to do a work that is far beyond your ability. But this only happens when you make things right on the inside and you are no longer hindered by the expectations of man.

Remember, God says, *"I have set before thee an open door, and no man can shut it"* (Revelation 3:8).

Door Number Four:
The Door the Church Must Open

Peter realized this was no dream. It really happened! And while he was shaking his head in amazement, he went to Mary's house—the one who was the mother of John Mark.

The home was filled with people who were still praying for Peter's release. Then, when he knocked on the door, a young woman named Rhoda stepped out into the courtyard to see who it was.

The Bible records, *"she knew Peter's voice"* (Acts 12:14), but was so excited to tell everyone of his release, she ran inside and left him standing there.

When Rhoda told the prayer warriors who had arrived, they said, *"Thou art mad. But she constantly affirmed that it was even so. Then said they, It is his angel"* (verse 15). They thought she had seen a ghost!

But Peter continued knocking: and when they opened the door and saw him, "they were astonished" (verse 16).

The message of the fourth door is that the church door must always remain open. If you are praying for someone's deliverance, why keep them waiting outside? Let the door swing wide and welcome them in.

The Lord who set Peter free, will do the same for you. Open the four doors of deliverance and see how God will perform His best work.

CHAPTER 4

DON'T BE A GAMBLER

Then said Jesus, Father, forgive them;
for they know not what they do. And they
parted his raiment, and cast lots.

– LUKE 23:34

Are you one of those individuals who loves to take a chance? Do you buy lottery tickets? What about trips to Las Vegas or a nearby casino?

In the last chapter we saw how the Bible speaks of the number four—and there is even more. Let me tell you about four soldiers who gambled for the clothing of Christ during the crucifixion. It must be significant since it is recorded in all four gospels.

The soldiers who nailed Christ to the cross, *"took his garments, and made four parts, to every soldier a part; and also his coat: now the coat was without seam, woven from the top throughout"* (John 19:23). See also Matthew 27:35; Mark 15:24; Luke 23:24.

The garment Jesus wore was "without seam"—meaning it was woven with one thread from top to bottom.

Since this was a beautiful piece of cloth, the soldiers didn't want to tear it, so they decided to gamble for its possession. The Bible tells us, *"They said therefore among themselves, Let us not rend it, but cast lots for it, whose it shall be"* (John 19:24).

RIGHT ON TIME

The Son of God, conceived of the Holy Ghost and born of a virgin, was sent from heaven. When He appeared, a day of destiny was birthed. It was a plan orchestrated by God long before man existed on this earth.

It is amazing that Jesus was sent to earth at a specific time for a specific purpose. He was born right on time—not early, nor late, but precisely on God's schedule. Let me tell you why.

The Romans gained control of Israel and had built a system of roads for travel. (Daniel 9:25 tells us how the streets of Jerusalem would be built again.)

There was one primary common language spoken at this time—Greek. In fact, all 27 books of the New Testament were written in Greek. So whether a person lived in Italy, Jerusalem, Crete, or Ephesus, he or she could read the scriptures.

It is also important to know that the Jews (even though they did not accept Christ) believed the Messiah would one day appear. Remember, the wise men who came to Bethlehem from Asia, Syria, and Iraq, knew what scripture said and they were looking for Him.

When God sent His Son to earth, everything was ready for His appearance.

The "seventy sevens" of Daniel 9 tells us how many years (490) it would be before the Messiah would come.

When God sent His Son to earth, everything was ready for His appearance.

THE DARKEST OF DAYS

Through natural eyes, Jesus was born during tumultuous times. The spiritual situation in Israel was the worst it had ever been. The Romans had taken total control. Even the high priests, Ananas and Caiaphas, were not true spiritual leaders. Herod had removed the real high priest and placed these two men in charge. Not only was the priesthood corrupt, but so were the moneychangers. They were selling blemished, unfit sacrifices to the people and overcharging for them.

It was also a dark day politically. If Herod suspected you were endangering his power, you were as good as dead. Remember, he felt threatened when Jesus was born and killed thousands of baby boys.

Economically, things were no better. The people were taxed continually, and the Roman soldiers could plunder what they wanted from your home, garden, or fields.

Those who had physical needs were outcasts from society. Leprosy and blood diseases were rampant and anyone with severe illness was cast aside to die.

However, the Romans tolerated Jewish traditions and allowed the Pharisees, Sadducees, and Sanhedrin Council to operate—and we know how they felt about Christ!

So Jesus was born at the perfect moment on God's calendar, but the worst of times in Israel.

PROPHECIES FULFILLED

When the Romans pronounced the death penalty, it was usually carried out by crucifixion—a slow, painful, public execution on a wooden cross or a tree.

Yet, hundreds of years earlier, God inspired the writers of the Old Testament to write an amazing description of what took place at Calvary:

- He was crucified with criminals (Isaiah 53:12; Matthew 27:35).

- He was given vinegar and gall for thirst (Psalm 26:21; Matthew 27:35).

- His side was pierced (Zechariah 12:10: John 19:34).

- None of His bones were broken (Psalm 34:20; John 19:33-36).

WHY WERE THEY GAMBLING?

When Jesus died, it was the only day in history that man, God, and the devil agreed —Jesus had to be put to death. Three worlds witnessed the crucifixion—those present in Jerusalem, the demons in hell, and the angels in heaven.

Three worlds witnessed the crucifixion— those present in Jerusalem, the demons in hell, and the angels in heaven.

While Christ was dying and the soldiers were gambling for His garments. I'm sure there were those watching who wondered, "Why don't you give His belongings to His mother? Or to His disciples? Why take a dying man's clothes?"

Let me explain why.

There was a certain garment worn by Jewish priests or a rabbi. This robe, or covering for the shoulders was carefully made and of great value. This is why the Roman soldiers were careful not to tear this particular item of clothing.

Remember, Jesus and His entire earthly family were Jews—the seed of Abraham, Isaac, and Jacob, and descendants from the line of David. The Jewish people called Him "Rabbi."

It is also essential to understand that no one was allowed to speak or teach at a synagogue unless they were a rabbi. Jesus journeyed from town to town and spoke in synagogues—which meant He had an education which prepared Him for this honor.

During this time, a person could not be named a rabbi until age 30—the exact age Jesus began His public ministry. It wasn't by accident.

So, being a rabbi and teaching in the synagogues, Jesus would have owned and worn a Jewish prayer shawl called a "tallit."

THE HEM OF HIS GARMENT

Today, you can see these shawls being worn by many

of the Jews who come to pray at the Western Wall—and orthodox Jews drape this garment across their back and wear it wherever they go. This dates back to the time God told Moses, *"Speak unto the children of Israel, and bid them that they make them fringes in the borders of their garments throughout their generations, and that they put upon the fringe of the borders a ribband of blue: And it shall be unto you for a fringe, that ye may look upon it, and remember all the commandments of the Lord, and do them; and that ye seek not after your own heart and your own eyes, after which ye use to go a whoring; That ye may remember, and do all my commandments, and be holy unto your God"* (Numbers 15:38-40).

Everything on this shawl has to be perfect, and each part has a special meaning—the color of the dye, the thread (seamless), the tassels, and the fringe. For example, there are 613 tassels, one for each commandment God gave His people.

Rabbis have worn these prayer shawls for centuries— and some of them flow all the way down to the ground like a long coat, covering the back and front.

The knots in the fringes are also meaningful. When tied together, each has special significance. One represents Jehovah Jireh (My Provider), another Jehovah Rophe (My Healer), etc.

In the New Testament we read the story of a woman with an issue of blood who pressed through a crowd of people to reach Jesus. Scripture records how she *"came behind him, and touched the hem of his garment: For she said within herself, If I may but touch his garment, I shall be whole"* (Matthew 9:20:21).

> *This woman knew enough about the Old Testament prophecies that if she just touched the fringes (tassels) of His robe, she would be healed.*

This woman knew enough about the Old Testament prophecies that if she just touched the fringes (tassels) of His robe, she would be healed. And she was!

NOT THE SHAWL, BUT THE SAVIOR

As the Roman soldiers led Jesus to Calvary, they put a crown of thorns on His head, a purple robe of royalty on His body, and mocked Him as a king. But when they reached the cross, they removed all of His clothing except for this one, seamless garment.

Then the Roman guards, knowing it was too expensive to tear apart and wanting to make some money, said to each other, *" Let us not rend it, but cast lots for it, whose it shall be"* (John 19:24). This was in direct fulfillment of the prophecy: *"They part my garments among them, and cast lots upon my vesture"* (Psalm 22:18).

Perhaps they thought, "This garment has some special properties—maybe it will heal people."

But that piece of cloth never healed again. People may have touched it, but nothing happened. Why? Because it wasn't the fringes or the prayer shawl. It was the Man inside the garment. It was Jesus the Healer!

Those who witnessed the crucifixion—and satan himself—didn't understand that three days later, Christ would be resurrected. He rose from the grave in the power of the Holy Ghost.

After completing His ministry on earth, Jesus ascended to heaven where He sits at the right hand of God, ready to make intercession for you and me.

DON'T GAMBLE WITH YOUR SOUL

When I survey the world situation today, I see the same darkness—politically, economically, and spiritually. It's a repeat of what happened 2,000 years ago.

This is why I believe we are nearing the time when God will give the signal to Gabriel to blow the trumpet. It will be the grand and glorious moment when *"the Lord himself shall descend from heaven with a shout, with the voice of the archangel, and with the trump of God: and the dead in Christ shall rise first: Then we which are alive and remain shall be caught up together with them in the clouds, to meet the Lord in the air: and so shall we ever be with the Lord"* (1 Thessalonians 4:16-17).

Are you ready to meet the Lord? Or will you be left behind? When it comes to eternity, don't gamble with your soul.

CHAPTER 5

HAVE YOU EVER BEEN TO LODEBAR?

*Then king David sent, and fetched him out of
the house of Machir, the son of Ammiel, from Lodebar.*
– 2 SAMUEL 9:5

Perhaps there has been a time in your life when you felt lonely and isolated—as if you were surrounded by darkness and couldn't talk to anyone. Maybe the situation was so desperate that you thought you were the only person alive, and no one could help you.

The Bible describes such a place—and it is called Lodebar.

Let's go back in time. In the battle of Gilboa, the Philistines defeated Israel and King Saul committed suicide (1 Samuel 31:4).

David ascended to the throne and one day asked if

there was anyone remaining in Saul's family. He wanted to show that person some godly kindness in honor of Jonathan—Saul's son and David's friend who was killed in the same Gilboa battle.

When David made his request, a servant from Saul's household named Ziba was present, and told him, *"Jonathan hath yet a son, which is lame on his feet"* (2 Samuel 9:3).

David asked, "Where is he?" To which Ziba answered, *"Behold, he is in the house of Machir, the son of Ammiel, in Lodebar"* (verse 4).

Immediately, David sent for him.

A TWISTED LIFE

Lodebar in the Hebrew means a "place of no communication" or "no words." *Lo* means "no" and *debar* means "word"—a place of darkness.

> **Have you ever been in a situation where you felt no one could help you?**

Let me ask again. Have you ever been in a situation where you felt no one could help you?

When the son of Jonathan came before David, the Bible describes how the man *"fell on his face, and did reverence. And David said, Mephibosheth. And he answered, Behold thy servant!"* (2 Samuel 9:6).

58

Me-phi-bo-sheth—now that's a real tongue twister; but his name was not nearly as twisted as his life.

Scripture records that his father, Jonathan, was strong, virile, and handsome. Since sons often take on the same characteristics as their dad, he was surely in line to become a future king. But in Mephibosheth, we find a bruised victim with broken ankles and deformed limbs.

At one time he lived in a royal palace, but now he was nothing more than a deposed and maimed prince from a house of fallen kings—living in exile in a lonely land.

This man lost his birthright and even his possible throne and kingdom without uttering a single word or doing one evil deed. He was just a frightened boy when he was sent to Lodebar.

Mephibosheth could only dream about what might have been, or perhaps listen to stories of his grandfather, King Saul, the first king of all Israel. If only his father, Jonathan, had not been killed, how different things would be.

IT WASN'T FAIR

It's amazing how brokenness in one area of our life can rob us of our rightful success and imprison us in a valley of regret. A place like Lodebar, a silent location where no one can hear our pain or ease our sorrow—where there is no help and no one is listening.

Mephibosheth could have risen to great heights, but the problem he faced was beyond his control. There was nothing wrong with him mentally. His mind could command his legs to walk but they would not respond. Oh, how he wished he could be like everyone else, but he was crippled.

> *We can be left silenced and hopeless—thinking about what should have been.*

You may not be able to fully relate to Mephibosheth's physical handicap, but each one of us has a certain degree of dysfunction that can lead us to Lodebar. We can be left silenced and hopeless—thinking about what should have been.

The infirmity of Mephibosheth was not a condition he was born with. Picture this healthy boy at age five, arising from his bed in the palace, having breakfast, and playing in the courtyard. His private nurse dressed him and perhaps he hoped that his dad and granddad would come home from the war that day.

His nurse then heard the terrible news. Jonathan and Saul had been killed! Everyone must flee for their lives. She grabbed the young boy and began to run from the palace with him in her arms. In their haste, as they fled, *"he fell, and became lame"* (2 Samuel 4:4). Both of his ankles and legs were broken, and he became a cripple for life.

It was not fair. This child didn't deserve such a future. Yet, it was an event from which he never recovered.

HURTING AND WOUNDED

I have met people who although they have not been physically dropped, the results seem to be the same. They complain:

- I could have done so much more with my life, but somebody dropped me.

- I am emotionally handicapped because somebody dropped me.

- I can't work for the Lord because somebody dropped me.

- You don't know what I've been through because somebody dropped me.

- I am in this dark place because somebody dropped me.

Mephibosheth's friends were few and far between. Children no longer played with him. What do you think this isolation did to his self-esteem?

HIDDEN SCARS

Sadly, I believe that in some cases the church has damaged people by telling them if they come to the altar, become a member, pay tithes, and join the choir, everything will be alright.

Without a total spiritual transformation, we can remain wounded for the rest of our lives.

The truth is, without a total spiritual transformation, we can remain wounded for the rest of our lives.

Friend, some things just won't disappear without divine intervention. If you were abused as a child, rejected, perhaps even raped, this is still inside you. It's all festering there—and you feel unloved, hated, forgotten, shut out, with invisible wounds, even physical, emotional, or spiritual problems. These are hidden scars and you are a trapped in Lodebar.

But I have wonderful news for you. The King of kings is calling your name! Jesus, the Savior and the Healer will take you right out of that dark place. Remember, God does His best work at night.

RESTORED TO THE KINGDOM

David asked to meet Mephibosheth and said to him, *"Fear not: for I will surely shew thee kindness for Jonathan thy father's sake, and will restore thee all the land of Saul thy father; and thou shalt eat bread at my table continually"* (2 Samuel 9:7).

What was the man's response. He wanted to know why the king should pay attention to a *"dead dog"* such as he felt he was (verse 8).

David called in Ziba, Saul's servant, and said to him:

I have given unto thy master's son all that pertained to Saul and to all his house. Thou therefore, and thy sons, and thy servants, shall till the land for him, and thou shalt bring in the fruits, that thy master's son may have food to eat: but Mephibosheth thy master's son shall eat bread always at my table. Now Ziba had fifteen sons and twenty servants.

Then said Ziba unto the king, According to all that my lord thy kind hath commanded his servant, so shall thy servant do. As for Mephibosheth, said the king, he shall eat at my table, as one of the king's sons. And Mephibosheth had a young son, whose name was

Micha. And all that dwelt in the house of Ziba
were servants unto Mephibosheth.

So Mephibosheth dwelt in Jerusalem: for he
did eat continually at the king's table; and was
lame on both his feet (2 Samuel 9:9-13).

Mephibosheth is no longer a five year old boy. He is
a grown man with a wife and son of his own.

But remember what happened at the beginning of this
story. David asked Ziba to go and find this man.
Mephibosheth was called to the palace; he did not come
on his own!

What a marvelous truth. Many are called but they are
unable to enter the King's house because of their
infirmities and brokeness.

YOUR NEW POSITION

You may need to rescue someone from the dark
valley of silence and oppression and help to set them
free.

Saul's servant is like the Holy Spirit of God. He
comes to clear our minds of fear and doubt, to lift us up
and bring us to the place we need to be. Ziba had to carry
Mephibosheth to the palace of David.

Many are in the wrong location, consumed by alcohol

or mind-numbing drugs, engaged in sexual misconduct, eaten up by jealousy and hatred, lying on the floor and unable to rise. They have no self-worth and no destiny.

What about you? No matter how wounded or handicapped you may be, Jesus is calling. By the world's standards, you are considered a failure, but there is a place of honor reserved for you at the King's table. Starting right now, you can enjoy the blessings and promises from the royal palace.

Mephibosheth began to receive food he didn't have to labor for. He was now a prince among princes. This was his new life—and he belonged!

Friend, your position can overcome your condition.

Perhaps you are an elder, a choir member, or a Sunday school teacher, but yet you are still hurting from hidden wounds and childhood scars.

Jesus is seeking you out and is waiting for you to be seated at His heavenly banquet. Though you are weak, He is strong. Don't allow your past to destroy what God has for your future.

Today, the Lord has a new life prepared just for you. Say goodbye to the silence and darkness of Lodebar. Get ready for the Son to shine once more.

CHAPTER 6

DARKNESS PROVIDED HIS COVER

*There was a man of the Pharisees, named
Nicodemus, a ruler of the Jews: The same came to Jesus
by night, and said unto him, Rabbi, we know that thou
art a teacher come from God: for no man can do these
miracles that thou doest, except God be with him.*

– JOHN 3:1-2

Nicodemus was filled with questions.

Yes, he was a member of the Jewish leadership known as the Sanhedrin Council. Yes, he was one of the wealthiest men in all of Jerusalem. Yes, he had attended the best schools and his education was second to none in all of Israel, but Nicodemus wanted to know something more.

Here was a man who sat daily with the religious elite.

He was a member of their councils. They would meet and discuss what was written in the Torah. They even had debated and tried to resolve questions of the law. "What does God say about this?" What does scripture mean concerning that?"

This scholar was as much at home in the temple as he was in his own home located in the high-end real estate section of Jerusalem. Nicodemus had education, financial status and a seat on the highest court in the land, but still he had questions—and he came in the dark cover of night to find his answers.

"MY FATHER'S HOUSE"?

Nicodemus had recently seen a tall suntanned Nazarene in the temple. He taught with authority and responded to questions no one else would even try to answer. His name was Jesus (Yeshua) from Nazareth.

Jesus was called by the common folk Messiah, Son of God, Healer, Rabbi, Teacher, Chosen One.

Nicodemus was in the temple the day that this Man took a braided whip and ran the moneychangers off Solomon's porch. He heard Jesus call them a den of thieves. He listened as Jesus called the temple "My Father's House." How could any man say that? He had plenty of questions.

It was nighttime when he slipped away to find his answers. No one knew his plans—not his family, and certainly not his friends and cohorts on the Sanhedrin Council. They would not understand. How could a leader of the Supreme Court over all of Israel even try to talk to this uneducated, rogue evangelist from Nazareth? What good could come of such a meeting? How would this encounter help Nicodemus?

How could a leader of the Supreme Court over all of Israel even try to talk to this uneducated, rogue evangelist from Nazareth?

"Don't Be Frightened"

Jesus and His disciples had settled in for the night. Those traveling with Him had prepared the evening meal and they were sitting around the campfire discussing the activities that occurred during the day.

Peter said, "Did you see those demons run when Jesus spoke to them?"

"Yes" answered John, the youngest disciple. "I saw leprosy leave men's bodies and their skin become clean and pure."

James commented, "So many people just want to

touch Him. Have you ever seen anything like this before?"

"No, never" the other disciples chimed in. More wood was added to the fire.

Then, out of the dark shadows walked a well-dressed figure. The disciples discerned quickly he was a man of authority—a scholar perhaps.

They were startled, and the noise was quickly silenced.

> *"Don't be frightened," said Nicodemus. "I will do you no harm. I am here to speak to Jesus."*

"Don't be frightened," said Nicodemus. "I will do you no harm. I am here to speak to Jesus."

At the mention of His name, Jesus looked up and motioned for Nicodemus to sit by Him. The disciples and other followers of Jesus were in awe.

"I am Nicodemus, a member of the council and I have come to ask you some questions."

BORN AGAIN?

Jesus did not answer, but His glance into the eyes of Nicodemus said, "It is alright. Ask Me what you will.

He began, *"Rabbi, we know that thou art a teacher come from God: for no man can do these miracles that thou doest, except God be him"* (John 3:2).

Nicodemus was fully aware of Jesus' ministry. Perhaps he had seen the Lord wipe away the blindness from someone's eyes or watched as He told a cripple man to rise and walk. He may have even heard Jesus say, "Go your way. Your sins are forgiven."

This man had first hand knowledge, but the Lord still did not react—not even taking the time to say "Hello" or "How are you?"

Jesus simply looked at Nicodemus and said, *"Verily, verily, I say unto thee, Except a man be born again, he cannot see the kingdom of God"* (verse 3).

The Lord knew His assignment. He knew why His Father God sent Him into this world—to seek and save those who were lost, to heal and deliver.

BEING BORN OF THE SPIRIT

Instead of talking with Nicodemus about his good works as a member of the Sanhedrin, or telling the man to pray or fast at the temple on Holy Days, Jesus got right to the point, telling him that he must be born again.

Jesus got right to the point, telling him that he must be born again.

This statement stunned this scholarly man, and he

asked, *"How can a man be born when he is old? Can he enter the second time into his mother's womb, and be born?"* (verse 4).

Nicodemus was skeptical, thinking, "This cannot be. We can't be born again. This is not going to happen."

The disciples sat and listened in stunned silence. They were just as bewildered as Nicodemus. They had never heard Jesus teach like this before.

Jesus looked at Nicodemus and softly reiterated His first statement. *"Verily, verily, I say unto thee, Except a man be born of water and of the Spirit, he cannot enter into the kingdom of God. That which is born of the flesh is flesh; and that which is born of the Spirit is spirit. Marvel not that I said unto thee, Ye must be born again"* (John 3:5-7).

Nicodemus thought about that statement. "Born of water"—that means a natural birth from a mother's womb. "Born of Spirit"—that means from the inside. "My spirit man must be born again—which tells me God must have something to do with this."

A NEW HEART

Jesus explained that being born again in spirit means a newborn heart that accepts the things of God from heaven. What happens on earth has nothing to do with it.

You can't "wish" or "earn" a new heart—and you certainly can't create one. There is only way. God must do the work!

Nicodemus thought man could solve his own problems, but Jesus plainly told him the transformation must be done by the Spirit of God.

Those words hit Nicodemus hard, and his thoughts were racing. He asked the Lord, *"How can these things be?"* (verse 9).

Jesus looked at this man and questioned, *"Art thou a master of Israel, and knowest not these things?"* (verse 10). And He continued, *"If I have told you earthly things, and ye believe not, how shall ye believe, if I tell you of heavenly things?"* (verse 12).

> *Nicodemus thought it was the person who did the work, but Jesus explained it was God—and how redemption is available to all people.*

Nicodemus thought it was the person who did the work, but Jesus explained it was God—and how redemption is available to all people.

FOREVER CHANGED

At that point Jesus presented the plan of salvation to

Nicodemus as clearly as it has ever been stated: *"For God so loved the world, that he gave his only begotten Son, that whosoever believeth in him should not perish, but have everlasting life"* (John 3:16).

What was the motive behind the new birth? The love of God. Not only to the children of Israel but to all men of all nations.

Nicodemus finally understood.

Now he knew that Jesus was the Son of God who did not come to earth to condemn the world, but to save it.

The man who came in the darkness of night received his answer. Now he knew that Jesus was the Son of God who did not come to earth to condemn the world, but to save it.

From that moment forward, Nicodemus was a born again believer, a follower of Christ.

On the day Jesus was crucified, Nicodeums was there with Joseph of Arimathaea. These two men oversaw the burial of Christ and helped place His body in the tomb (John 19:38-40).

Three days later, the news was spreading: "Jesus is alive. He has risen from the dead!"

Nicodemus was rejoicing. He had accepted Christ as his Messiah. He had been born again and heaven was waiting for him.

Like this man, you may be in the darkest moment of your journey with many unanswered questions, but by simple faith and belief, Jesus will give you His light, His love, and His everlasting life.

CHAPTER 7

WHAT IS YOUR POINT OF NEED?

Then said I, Woe is me! for I am undone;
because I am a man of unclean lips.
— ISAIAH 6:5

Isaiah came to the Temple at a time of crisis. King Uzziah had died and he was very concerned about the kingdom sliding into darkness and rebellion.

Some Bible historians claim that Isaiah was related to Uzziah, perhaps his nephew. Regardless, Isaiah loved King Uzziah very much and was now seeking the Lord on behalf of Israel.

The king had been a godly ruler, leading the people in the path of righteousness, and Isaiah was extremely concerned over the transition of power and what would happen next.

While he was in the Temple praying, Isaiah saw a heavenly vision. As he describes it, *"I saw also the Lord sitting upon a throne, high and lifted up, and his train filled the temple. Above it stood the seraphims: each one had six wings; with twain he covered his face, and with twain he covered his feet, and with twain he did fly. And one cried unto another, and said, Holy, holy, is the Lord of hosts: the whole earth is full of his glory"* (Isaiah 6:1-3).

This picture of angelic beings around the throne of God almost defies our imagination.

When we read and study the scriptures and learn of visions and miracles, it is hard for our human mind to fully comprehend the magnitude of what God is doing. This is why we must enter into the spirit realm of the Father and receive what He is trying to tell us.

I KNOW IT HAPPENED

Without personally witnessing the event, it is difficult for us to grasp the wonders God performed. But by faith and the assurance of the Word, we can claim these events as truth. For example:

- I didn't see the Red Sea open. But I know it happened.

- I didn't see the water flow out of the rock. But I know it happened.

- I didn't see the Jordan River roll back. But I know it happened.

- I didn't see Jesus feed the five thousand. But I know it happened.

- I didn't see Lazarus come out of the grave. But I know it happened.

A MIST OF GLORY

You and I didn't see these angelic hosts that Isaiah described, so it is hard for us to imagine what they really looked like.

These angels are referred to over thirty times in the Bible and are detailed as creatures of phenomenal beauty.

The prophet Ezekiel and John the disciple also wrote about these heavenly beings which encircle the throne of God. These angels are referred to over thirty times in the Bible and are detailed as creatures of phenomenal beauty.

Isaiah also tells us that in his vision, the room *"was*

filled with smoke" (verse 4). This is not smoke as you and I might recognize, but it is like the "Shekinah Glory" of God that is always symbolic of His majesty.

This smoke could have been called the "glory mist." Perhaps you have attended a service where this divine mist—such as the smell of roses—was evident.

I have sat in anointed meetings where a mist, or presence, surrounds the altar to such an extent that healings, miracles, and salvations have occurred in great numbers.

And just when we think it can't get any better, the Lord will send another wind, another shower of His glory that exceeds what we have already experienced.

Never be amazed at what God can do, because *"Eye hath not seen, nor ear heard, neither have entered into the heart of man, the things which God hath prepared for them that love him"* (1 Corinthians 2:9).

The Lord has promised, *"...no good thing will he withhold from them that walk uprightly"* (Psalm 84:11).

Today, I am totally convinced that God is looking for people like you and me who will stand for Him and say, "Lord, here I am. Use me."

"WOE IS ME"

Isaiah was just such a man. It was not what he

witnessed in his vision that is so significant, it is how he responded to what he saw.

His reaction was one of total unworthiness. He looked up to God and cried, *"Woe is me! For I am undone; because I am a man of unclean lips, and I dwell in the midst of a people of unclean lips: for mine eyes have seen the King, the Lord of hosts"* (Isaiah 6:5).

> *If he had been living today, Isaiah would have probably said, "I live in a corrupt society. I rub shoulders every day with sinners of this world."*

If he had been living today, Isaiah would have probably said, "I live in a corrupt society. I rub shoulders every day with the sinners of this world. I feel filthy and impure."

Isaiah was a godly man—perhaps the most righteous of all the prophets. He totally understood the covenant of Abraham, Isaac, and Jacob. But as we read these verses, we see how Isaiah was overwhelmed as he came into the presence of God.

A SACRED MOMENT

You may meet a pastor, evangelist, or teacher, but no human encounter can compare to standing before the living God and sensing who you are.

Can you imagine what it would be like to walk into God's house as Isaiah did—and you were the only person there? Just you and the Lord.

When you enter the Temple you see God. He is high and lifted up, sitting on His throne, and His robe is like the train of a bride's wedding dress which fills the entire sanctuary.

In the book of Revelation we read how John saw a vision of heaven, but Isaiah's vision was in the place where he went to worship, the Temple of Solomon.

It was here that the presence of God filled the entire house. There was not a nook or cranny, an aisle or pew, or anything left untouched.

Can you envision coming into your house of worship and God being there? What a sacred moment! Everywhere you walk, you are covered and filled by His presence.

This was the case with Isaiah. But thankfully, he was prepared for such a glorious meeting.

A COAL FROM THE ALTAR

What about you? Are you ready for an encounter with the living God? You had better be!

Such an event would take most people by surprise. You have just finished a busy day of anger, frustration, problems, and fear. There are complications at every turn with your family and your job. Plus, the pressure of the world has rubbed off on you. As a result, you said or did something you now regret.

Even though you are not a sinner, you still feel unworthy.

Have you noticed that God often comes to meet us at the most inappropriate time? He shows up when we really don't want Him to be there.

> *Have you noticed that God often comes to meet us at the most inappropriate time?*

Isaiah must have said, "Lord, I came here to pray and talk with You, but I didn't realize You would be here personally." As a result, he didn't feel worthy to be in God's midst.

Thankfully, there comes a time when it is not important what you have (or have not) done. It's all about what the Lord has done, and at this point God's presence and your sense of unworthiness meet.

In Isaiah's case, the Lord commissioned an angel to visit him and meet him at his point of need. As scripture records, *"Then flew one of the seraphims unto me, having a live coal in his hand, which he had taken with the tongs from off the altar: And he laid it upon my mouth, and said, Lo, this hath touched thy lips; and thine iniquity is taken away, and thy sin purged"* (Isaiah 6:6-7).

LOOKING IN A MIRROR

Many believers love God and have tasted His goodness. We desire His blessings and even want His correction if necessary—but only to the point of our comfort zone. It seems we can't enter into God's presence as Isaiah did with total assurance. Although we sense His nearness, we feel removed from Him.

> *We desire His blessings and even want His correction if necessary—but only to the point of our comfort zone.*

Why does this happen? The only thing that separates us from God is sin.

Your mother, your father, and your teachers all said you were a good kid. They may have implied you were perfect and you believed them. Before long you found yourself looking in the mirror for a halo, but it was nowhere to be found.

Then God shows up and His glory is all around you. This is when you see yourself as you truly are—with all your faults and imperfections. In His presence He immediately reveals your true self. You see things you didn't even realize, and you want to hide. It's no wonder you feel so unworthy.

WHAT DO YOU NEED?

Friend, when the Lord appears on the scene, don't run away. It is only when you linger in His presence that you can become like Him. He will meet you at your point of need:

- Do you need salvation? Get in **His** presence.

- Do you need a healing? Get in **His** presence.

- Do you have a financial need? Get in **His** presence.

Isaiah said that he was a man of unclean lips (verse 5) but the angel put a hot coal on those lips and cleansed them (verse 6).

- If Isaiah had an impure heart, the angel would have touched his heart.

- If Isaiah had an impure mind, God would have touched his mind.

- If he had been lame, He would have placed the hot coals on his lameness.

In order to have His touch on our lives we must stay around the anointing and be infused by His Spirit.

If Isaiah had run from the Temple, God would not have touched him.

THE GREAT TRANSFORMATION

The Lord created worship as an instrument of restoration. Why worship and praise? It does not change God—it changes you!

As we enter into His presence, the Lord wants to restore and bring us to our rightful place. But we must come before God with our whole heart. Our time of worship must never be a quick prayer or brief praise. That won't suffice. We need to grow in God and experience the depth of His Spirit—staying in His presence until we are transformed into His likeness and image.

It is impossible to experience an encounter like Isaiah had and not be forever changed.

It is impossible to experience an encounter like Isaiah had and not be forever changed.

For too long we have seen people enter the house of God and sing, shout, and praise Him. But when they leave the sanctuary they continue to live like the world.

It's time to become serious about true worship—praying *through*, until you touch God and He touches you.

DRAWN TO HIM

The Lord desires to draw us to Himself.

Have you ever seen what happens when you place a magnet on a plate of metal shavings? Those tiny shavings will literally crawl and jump over each other to get to the magnet—and they will cling there.

As we worship the Lord we become magnetized and drawn to Him. Christ is being fully formed in us and we become like Jesus.

When we read about the angels encircling the throne they are worshiping God, crying, "Holy, Holy, Holy."

The focal point must never be on you or your problems. Instead, take you eyes off yourself and look at the Lord.

God is saying, "I know your imperfections, your inabilities, your pains and your hurts. Just stay in My midst and I will make you brand new. As Isaiah writes, *"They that wait upon the Lord shall renew their strength; they shall mount up with wings as eagles; they shall run, and not be weary; and they shall walk, and not faint"* (Isaiah 40:31).

Remain in God's presence until He covers you with

His righteousness and holiness. He will not only give you a vision of Himself, but will provide direction for your future.

"Whom Shall I Send?"

King Uzziah had died, and Isaiah went to the Temple to pray that God would send the right person to provide moral leadership for the nation.

After this divine encounter, he heard the voice of the Almighty ask, *"Whom shall I send, and who will go for us?"* (Isaiah 6:8).

Only then was Isaiah able to say, *"Here am I: send me"* (verse 8).

How will you respond?

CHAPTER 8

"I WILL FEAR NO EVIL"

Yea though I walk through the valley of the shadow of death, I will fear no evil: for thou art with me; thy rod and thy staff they comfort me.

— PSALM 23:4

As a child in Sunday school you probably learned to quote at least a portion of the 23rd Psalm. It holds a timeless message for you and me.

David, the author of most of the psalms, spent his youth as a shepherd—and knew what it meant to love and care for his flock. He watched over them by day as they fed on the grasses, and corralled them at night so they would be safe.

In his hands were the tools of his trade, the rod to protect the flock from predators, and the staff (with a crook at the end) to help bring back a sheep that had strayed from the path of safety.

I can see David, after rounding up his flock and lying down for the night, saying, *"The Lord is my shepherd; I shall not want. He maketh me to lie down in green pastures: he leadeth me beside the still waters. He restoreth my soul: he leadeth me in the paths of righteousness for his name's sake"* (Psalm 23:1-3).

"IN THE WORD"

The reason this psalm is important is because God's Word has a vital message for each of us. We must study, speak, memorize, and renew our minds with His Word.

- In the Word there is healing
- In the Word there is peace
- In the Word there is joy
- In the Word there is understanding

In the Word is Jesus—and because of Him we no longer need to be afraid.

During these tumultuous times, the enemy is attacking us from all sides: right, left, front, rear, overhead, and underneath. So in order to combat the devil, we need to be bathed and soaked in scripture.

When satan attacks, a shout won't help you. You have to boldly confront him just as Jesus did, with the Word.

"IT IS WRITTEN"

Before Jesus began His public ministry, He was taken into the wilderness by the Spirit to be tested. He prepared for this temptation by fasting forty days and forty nights. As you can imagine, this left him in a state of hunger, which the devil quickly took advantage of.

When satan attacks, a shout won't help you. You have to boldly confront him as Jesus did, with the Word.

Satan taunted, *"If thou be the Son of God, command that these stones be made bread"* (Matthew 4:3).

Jesus answered by quoting from Deuteronomy 8:3: *"It is written, Man shall not live by bread alone, but by every word that proceedeth out of the mouth of God"* (Matthew 4:4).

He was saying, "It's in the Word."

Now it was time for the second test. Satan escorted the Lord to the Holy City, to the top of the Temple, and said, *"If thou be the Son of God, cast thyself down: for it is written [and here satan quoted from Psalm 91], He shall give his angels charge concerning thee: and in their hands they shall bear thee up, lest at any time thou dash thy foot against a stone"* (Matthew 4:6).

Jesus answered with another quotation from the Word (Deuteronomy 6:16): *"It is written again, Thou shalt not tempt the Lord thy God"* (Matthew 4:7).

Once more, the Lord used scripture.

Finally, satan took the Lord to the peak of a large mountain, pointing out all the earth's kingdoms and how marvelous they were. Then the devil offered, *"All these things will I give thee, if thou wilt fall down and worship me"* (verse 9).

Jesus refused satan with this blunt, but powerful statement: *"Get thee hence, Satan: for it is written, Thou shalt worship the Lord thy God, and him only shalt thou serve"* (Matthew 4:10).

Jesus defeated the devil the same way you and I can—with the Word.

There is an urgent need for men, women, and children everywhere to listen and hear what God is saying. You must not leave the work to your pastor or your church. In these critical days, you must become a lighthouse *personally* to those who desperately need help.

FACING THE DARKNESS

Like the psalmist, God desires for you to be able to say, *"Yea though I walk through the valley of the shadow of death, I will fear no evil: for thou art with me; thy rod and thy staff they comfort me"* (Psalm 23:4).

What a declaration of independence! This is an absolute truth from the Word of God.

You can face any danger, any darkness in your life, because of these five words: "I will fear no evil."

> *You can face any danger, any darkness in your life, because of these five words: "I will fear no evil."*

Come hell or high water, come sickness and disease, come bankruptcy, come divorce, come drugs, come alcohol or foe: "I will fear no evil."

I believe these words were written specifically for the times we are living in at this very moment. The Bible declares that in the last days there will be *distress of nations, with perplexity; the sea and the waves roaring; Men's hearts failing them for fear, and for looking after those things which are coming on the earth"* (Luke 21:25-26).

THE ROARING LION

Scripture predicted our present War on Terror. It tells how threats to our existence will saturate us to such an extent that we will become paralyzed by fear and feel overwhelmed and helpless.

What makes the difference between being caught and escaping? It all depends on your reaction to the roar.

Remember, we have been warned to: *"Be sober, be vigilant; because your adversary the devil, as a roaring lion, walketh about, seeking whom he may devour"* (1 Peter 5:8).

This parallels the lions who roam the jungles and roar to frighten and scare their prey so they can move in for the kill. Their targets may run, but they can't hide!

However, if you look closely at the scripture above, it says the devil is looking for those he *"may"* devour. This means there must be some of us he cannot devour.

What makes the difference between being caught and escaping? It all depends on your reaction to the roar.

If life bellows at you and you respond with utter terror and forget who you are in Christ (what He saved you from and your place in Him), then you will be a candidate to be devoured. But, if you remember *Whose* you are, when the enemy roars, you can look him in the eyes and demand, "Satan, get out of here. I am not afraid!"

While men's hearts are failing them for fear, as believers, we know it is simply a sign that something far greater is about to take place. As scripture tells us, *"And then shall they see the Son of man coming in a cloud with power and great glory. And when these things begin to come to pass, then look up, and lift up your heads; for your redemption draweth nigh"* (Luke 21:27-28).

PETRIFIED AND PARANOID

If you are like me, there are certain things that can shake you up and cause anxiety, but remember this:

- There is a difference in being concerned and being petrified.

- There is a difference in being careful and being intimidated.

- There is a difference in being cautious and being negative or paranoid.

Some people develop phobias which affect them to such an extent that they won't even leave their house. Fear prevents them from doing what is necessary to be free.

Think about this. When you are afraid, you can hardly speak or communicate your thoughts properly. In fact, it dominates your entire mental process. This is why the enemy loves for you to be consumed with worry and anxiety.

THE BIRTH OF TERRORISM

There are dangers, toils, and snares on every corner; trouble at work, problems at home, financial difficulties, jobs vanishing, kids being rebellious, husbands being unfaithful, wives leaving for another man.

In addition, we are dealing with terror escalating all over the world—not just Palestine and Pakistan, but from Great Britain to Indonesia. When we pick up the morning paper or watch the evening news we never know where evil will break out next.

Terrorism may have been new to the United States on September 11, 2001, but it has existed since Adam and Eve walked in the Garden of Eden.

Satan came to terrorize whomever he could.

THE SPIRIT OF FEAR

What we are truly facing is not hijacked airplanes, guns, or weapons of every description. This attack concerns fear—which is a spirit. And it is impossible to shoot or blow up a spirit!

Congress, the President, or war generals can do what they may, but the Bible clearly tells us there is a "spirit of fear."

In order to defeat this spirit, we must get on our knees and rebuke this evil attack against us, our families, the church, and our nation. We must cast it out!

Here's the exciting news. As a believer, you have been given the power to do just that: *"(For the weapons of our warfare are not carnal, but mighty through God to the pulling down of strong holds;) Casting down imaginations, and every high thing that exalteth itself against the knowledge of God, and bringing into captivity every thought to the*

> *In order to defeat this spirit, we must get on our knees and rebuke this evil attack against us, our families, the church, and our nation. We must cast it out!*

obedience of Christ" (2 Corinthians 10:4-5).

THE CHOICE IS OURS

The planes that were commandeered by the Islamic jihadists may have hit the trade towers and the Pentagon, but what the enemy really wanted to do was not just destroy the buildings or take the lives of innocent people: they desired to instill fear in our nation.

In some respects they succeeded, because millions became frightened of the future. But you and I have been given a choice. We are either going to live our lives in terror, or we are going to stand and declare, "I will fear no evil!"

> *We are either going to live our lives in terror, or we are going to stand and declare, "I will fear no evil!"*

Never forget that the devil pounces on fear like God moves on faith. Satan loves to take over your thoughts and actions. Every time a negative situation arises, the enemy is ready and waiting to plant seeds of discouragement and doubt. Far worse than the event itself is the fright and dread that rises up inside you. This makes you a candidate to be devoured.

But remember, *"God hath not given us the spirit of*

fear; but of power, and of love, and of a sound mind" (2 Timothy 1:7).

SHEEP NEED A SHEPHERD

When God refers to the church, He does not call us elephants, rhinos, eagles, or horses. No, He calls us sheep.

Most people dislike this comparison. They think of the phrase "dumb sheep," and would far rather be compared with a giant elephant, a tough-skinned rhino, a high-flying eagle, or a fast-running horse, But no, God called us, His children, sheep.

Sheep are intimidated, vulnerable, lacking in toughness, with no claws, unable to fight back, and must be led around. A man once told me, "I don't want to be a sheep. I'd prefer to be tough and in charge."

Yet the Lord stated, *"Behold, I send you forth as sheep in the midst of wolves"* (Matthew 10:16). He was saying, "Take no thought of where you are going."

Why would God tell us to be like sheep and not be afraid? Because sheep need a shepherd and Jesus is our Shepherd.

God's Son promises, *"I am the good shepherd, and know my sheep, and am known of mine. As the Father knoweth me, even so know I the Father: and I lay down my life for the sheep"* (John 10:14-15).

When the wolf, the lion, or the enemy prowls at your school, your job, or your home, the Shepherd is always there waiting to protect you.

"MY" SHEPHERD

The 23rd Psalm is a powerful, lethal weapon in the hands of every believer. It begins with a divine revelation of who God is—"my shepherd" (Psalm 21:1). And as a result you *"shall not want"* for anyone else.

The person who doesn't truly know who God is could easily be swayed into worshiping and glorifying the enemy. They might say, "Look at what this person did for me or made happen."

Before long the same individual you hold in high esteem may be a wolf in sheep's clothing. These are people with evil intentions who can bring utter chaos into your life.

I trust you can see why it is so vital that you understand who God is and the favor He is waiting to pour out on you.

Today I can testify to the fact that the Lord truly *is* my Shepherd—not *was, used to be, can be,* or *hope to be* in the future.

He is with me—on the airplane, in a boat, or in my car. Think of it. The same God who created the universe, allows me to have a personal Shepherd.

I can understand how I would be His—but this verse says He is *mine*. The scripture is not talking about groups, clubs, churches, or denominations, just me. If there were not another soul on this planet, He would still be *my* Shepherd.

> *The same God who created the universe, allows me to have a personal Shepherd.*

This makes me want to shout!

WHAT IS YOUR NEED?

David understood sheep to the extent that he knew how to help a ewe give birth to a little lamb. Because of his care and concern, there was an extremely strong bond established between the shepherd and his sheep.

Later, when David faced the Goliaths of his life, he would simply repeat what he already knew: "The Lord is my shepherd!"

Friend, the Shepherd will reveal Himself to you as you need Him:

- If you are thirsty, He will be water from a rock.

- If you are hungry, He will be manna from heaven.

- If you are sinking on shifting sand, He will be your Chief Cornerstone.

God will show up in a form you can relate to—and as a result you shall never want.

GREEN PASTURES

In the next few verses we see how the Lord takes charge. There are times when God *makes* you do something. *"He maketh me to lie down in green pastures"* (Psalm 23:2).

We may not have enough common sense to lie down on our own accord, but our heavenly Father knows what is best for us—and will force the issue.

Many times I have looked up to heaven and said, "Thank you Lord for taking charge. I was nervous and You calmed my fears. I couldn't sleep, and You gave me rest."

The Lord makes us lie down in pastures that are green and life-giving. Often we don't know how we reached such a place, but He teaches us to rest on abundant, fertile ground—not some barren, dry landscape. God not only blesses you, but makes you lie down in your blessings.

THE MIRACLE OF RESTORATION

Yes, God will give you direction, be He will also lead and guide you. As David writes, *"...he leadeth me beside the still waters"* (Psalm 23:2).

Whatever you're going through, He is out ahead, leading the way. All you have to do is walk in His footsteps and follow Him to where the waters are peaceful and tranquil.

If sheep are grazing near rushing water, they may wade in and drown. So the Good Shepherd leads His sheep by calm, still waters—those He knows they can handle.

The Good Shepherd leads His sheep by calm, still waters—those He knows they can handle.

When you follow His leading, you're ready for a special blessing. In the words of the psalmist, *"He restoreth my soul"* (Psalm 23:3).

- Even if I doubt
- Even if I fail
- Even if I become angry
- Even if I lose my job
- Even if I don't read my Bible
- Even if I fail to attend church as I should
- Even if I forget to fast and pray

When the enemy brought sickness and disease, the Great Physician was there to give you health and life.

List all the "even's" you can think of. But know this: God is ready and able to restore your soul.

Just when the devil thought he had you, God stepped in and performed a mighty miracle of restoration. When the enemy brought sickness and disease, the Great Physician was there to give you health and life.

YOUR HEAVENLY GPS

Not only will the Lord restore me, *"...he leadeth me in the paths of righteousness for his name's sake"* (Psalm 23:3).

God is your heavenly GPS and will keep you on the

right road. If you wander off course, He will lead you back to the right path. When you don't feel like being righteous, He will lead you to righteousness.

When you experience true salvation, you no longer do what you formerly desired because your body is now the temple of the Holy Ghost—and God's Spirit will lead you on the way that is right, pure, and just.

After your were born again perhaps you decided to go out and do something you knew was wrong, but God wouldn't let you. You called her but nobody answered. You went to meet him but the traffic made you turn back. This wasn't coincidence, it was the Almighty leading you in paths of righteousness to keep you from falling into sin.

KEEP ON WALKING!

The testimony of David can also be yours: *"Yea, though I walk through the valley of the shadow of death, I will fear no evil"* (Psalm 23:4).

As long as airplanes fly, I'm getting on board! As long as my car can run, I'm going. Why? Because I will fear no evil.

I may be walking through the dark valley and death is all around me, but I'm pushing through. I have places to go, people to reach with the Gospel, and lives who need to be delivered and healed by God's mighty power.

Stop listening to the voices of fear who tell you that if you eat a particular food you will get diabetes, develop cancer, have a heart attack and die. Yes, you have to use common sense, but don't give the enemy permission to terrorize you with what produces more health failures and death than any other cause—fear!

The valleys are very real, but God has chosen you to be part of a generation that will walk through the shadows.

Tell satan, "I'm filled with God's Spirit and I am not going to allow you to confuse me with doubt and despair." Let him know that a thousand may fall at your left and ten thousand on your right, but you are going to keep on walking!

The valleys are very real, but God has chosen you to be part of a generation that will walk through the shadows. Write these words on your computer, on your mirror, on your desk, and memorize them: "I will fear no evil!"

YOUR DEFENSE

The Almighty is with you in life and in death. This is

why you can tell your enemies, " Don't fool around with me because the Lord is on my side. If you try to fight, you will have to fight God because He is with me."

If God be for you, who can stand against you? There is no way your foes can win because the Lord's rod and staff are your protection.

Your Shepherd is never weak or passive—He will fight on your behalf. *"When the enemy shall come in like a flood, the Spirit of the Lord shall lift up a standard against him"* (Isaiah 59:19).

> *There is no way your foes can win because the Lord's rod and staff are your protection.*

You are not alone, so don't feel you constantly have to defend yourself. God is ready and able to take charge of your battles:

- He can fight cancer
- He can fight divorce
- He can fight bankruptcy
- He can fight injustice

If I am all by myself, I'd be easy to defeat. But when I get into my fighting position—down on my knees— and call on my Shepherd, no one can conquer me.

The Anointing

Today, call on Jesus and He will answer. Demons tremble at the very mention of His name. You will be able to say with David, *"Thou preparest a table before me in the presence of mine enemies"* (Psalm 23:5).

In other words, He will bless you while others are trying to do you harm.

In addition, the Lord will anoint your head with oil (verse 5). In both Old Testament times and during the life of Jesus, an honored guest was anointed with oil or perfumes.

I also learned that shepherds place oil on the heads of sheep so snakes won't bite them. They also put oil around a snake hole so the serpents will remain in their lair.

I'm glad the Bible tells us that the anointing of the Holy Spirit will protect us. What a gift from above!

Running Over!

With God's touch, get ready to rejoice. Shout with David, *"...my cup runneth over"* (verse 5).

As a result of the Lord's favor, you can say, *"Surely goodness and mercy shall follow me all the days of my life: and I will dwell in the house of the Lord for ever"* (verse 6).

Every time you look around, you will be pursued by God's blessings. They will not only follow you, but also your household—for the rest of your days!

Behind every shadow is God's goodness and mercy that will overtake you.

The enemy will roar, but when he does, look him straight in the face, point your finger at him and declare, "I will fear no evil."

CHAPTER 9

THE DARKEST STORM

For there stood by me this night the
angel of God, whose I am, and whom
I serve, Saying, Fear not, Paul...
– ACTS 27:23-24

H ave you ever been in a place so dark that you could not see your own hand right in front of your eyes?

What if you found yourself in such a situation because you were following God's direction? What if this meant being aboard a ship in turbulent seas where there was no sun, moon, or stars for fourteen days and you had not eaten? Yet, you were on a mission from the Almighty and He told you everything would be all right.

The darkest storm will sometimes hit when you least expect—and it can even arrive when you are in God's perfect will and on His timetable.

If you read the book of Acts you will understand how this is possible.

The Bounty Hunter

The apostle Paul, the man used by God to write most of our New Testament, was the new name for Saul—a Jew who once despised Christians.

Paul (Saul) was on a journey for the Sanhedrin Council. His job was to persecute followers of Christ, hunt them down, put them in jail, and even kill them. And Saul was good at his job.

One day Saul, the bounty hunter, came near to Damascus, a light brighter than the noonday sun shone down from heaven upon an unsuspecting Saul and knocked him to the ground. A voice from that light spoke to him and asked, "Why, Saul, are you persecuting me?"

Terrified, Saul wanted to know, "Who are you?"

Terrified, Saul wanted to know, "Who are you?"

And the Lord answered, *"I am Jesus whom thou persecutest"* (Acts 9:5). This was the very name Saul hated!

The story could be verified because those traveling with Saul also heard the same voice, but did not see the Man. Saul then brought up the question each one of us need to ask, *"Lord, what wilt thou have me to do?"* (verse 6).

TOTALLY TRANSFORMED

At that moment, Saul accepted Jesus as Lord and followed Christ. Totally blinded by the bright light, he was led to Damascus, and during this time of obscurity, deprived of his sight, he became a totally transformed individual.

Through a vision, the Lord led a disciple named Ananias to the place Saul was staying. Ananias said, *"Brother Saul, the Lord, even Jesus, that appeared unto thee in the way as thou camest, hath sent me, that thou mightest receive thy sight, and be filled with the Holy Ghost. And immediately there fell from his eyes as it had been scales: and he received sight forthwith, and arose, and was baptized"* (Acts 9:17-18).

With a new name and a new mission, Paul learned God's plan for his life. He was to take the gospel of Christ to the Gentiles, which he faithfully did.

ARRESTED AND DEPORTED

As you read the story of this great first century missionary, even though he was fulfilling God's will, the enemy was out to destroy him.

Paul completed his journey to Damascus where he preached Jesus as Savior and Lord. Then onto Jerusalem where he proclaimed Christ in the courts of Judea, to the Jews and the Gentiles.

Because Paul was caught in the temple preaching that Jesus was the Messiah, he was arrested and brought before King Agrippa.

Paul asked the king, "Do you not believe?"

King Agrippa and his sister Bernice had just heard Paul preach Jesus to them and the king answered, *"Almost thou persuadest me to be a Christian"* (Acts 26:28).

King Agrippa said to the governor, "This man might have been set free today, but he appealed to Caesar, so to Caesar he goes." Then he turned to the apostle and announced, "Paul you are going to Rome."

A HORRENDOUS VOYAGE

It is marvelous to know that the Lord brings us to the place He wants us to be. Remember that He promises, *"I will never leave thee, nor forsake thee"* (Hebrews 13:5).

God will launch us on a mission, but at times the journey may become black as night.

Paul was handed over to a centurion for the voyage to Rome. A ship was contracted and they began the long journey, stopping at various ports along the way.

They were in a hurry, but this was at the end of fall

and winter storms were already blowing. Some days the ship could barely move forward and they were far behind schedule.

Eventually the ship made it past Cyprus and into a port in Crete. Then, as they prepared to leave for one more leg of the journey, Paul told the centurion, *"Sirs, I perceive that this voyage will be with hurt and much damage, not only of the lading and ship, but also of our lives"* (Acts 27:10).

Obviously, Paul had received a word from the Lord.

The master of the ship, however, disregarded the advice and set sail for the next harbor. But no sooner had the vessel ventured out to sea, *"there arose against it a tempestuous wind, called Euroclydon* (verse 14)—a dark, cyclonic northeast storm which occurs in the Mediterranean.

The winds were so intense that no one could control the ship. They tried everything to keep the vessel from breaking up, including throwing valuable cargo overboard and tying ropes under the ship's belly.

> **The winds were so intense that no one could control the ship.**

There was no sun, moon, or stars for days on end. It was such a horrendous experience that their appetite for food, even life itself, was fading fast.

Now it was time for God to show up and do His best work!

WHAT ABOUT TOMORROW?

Paul had been quiet during this entire ordeal, but finally he stood in the midst of the terrified men and told them:

> *Sirs, ye should have hearkened unto me, and not have loosed from Crete, and to have gained this harm and loss. And now I exhort you to be of good cheer: for there shall be no loss of any man's life among you, but of the ship.*
>
> *For there stood by me this night the angel of God, whose I am, and whom I serve, Saying, Fear not, Paul; thou must be brought before Caesar: and, lo, God hath given thee all them that sail with thee. Wherefore, sirs, be of good cheer: for I believe God, that it shall be even as it was told me* (Acts 27:21-25).

However, the apostle did tell the 276 men on board that they would experience a total shipwreck.

HOPING FOR DAYLIGHT

After fourteen days of this terrible storm, around the

hour of midnight, the sailors sensed they were approaching land. They let down a measuring string and it read 120 feet. Shortly thereafter it read 90 feet. But since they were afraid they would run aground, they threw out four anchors and hoped for daylight.

The Bible records some of the sailors tried to jump ship, letting down the lifeboat—pretending they were going to throw more anchors over the bow (verses 30-31).

But Paul said to the centurion and to the soldiers, *"Except these abide in the ship, ye cannot be saved"* (verse 32). So the men cut the lines to the lifeboat and let it drift away.

A FINAL MEAL

When the sun was about to rise, Paul called everyone together and asked them to eat a good breakfast: *"This day is the fourteenth day that ye have tarried and continued fasting, having taken nothing. Wherefore I pray you to take some meat: for this is for your health: for there shall not an hair fall from the head of any of you"* (verses 33-34).

Next, Paul took some bread and gave thanks to the Lord in the presence of the men. The Bible tells us they were *"all of good cheer, and they also took some meat"* (verse 36).

This prepared them for the final blow. Since they thought this was probably the end of their voyage, everything was cast overboard and the ship was allowed to run ashore, as close to land as possible, before it would hit ground and finally break apart.

The soldiers had been told to *"kill the prisoners, lest*

_____
The word God gave Paul through the angel was totally fulfilled.
_____

any of them should swim out, and escape. But the centurion, willing to save Paul, kept them from their purpose; and commanded that they which could swim should cast themselves first into the sea, and get to land: And the rest, some on boards, and some on broken pieces of the ship (Acts 27:42-47).

So the word God gave Paul through the angel was totally fulfilled. No lives were lost. They miraculously survived the darkest storm.

CAST DOWN, BUT NOT DESTROYED

Friend, let me encourage you to stay close to a real man or woman of God such as the apostle Paul was. Listen to what the Lord is saying to them.

Yes there will be "Eurocyldons" along the way, but if you know Jesus, you will not remain in the storm-tossed seas.

This is why Paul was able to say, *"We are troubled on every side, yet not distressed; we are perplexed, but not in despair; persecuted, but not forsaken; cast down, but not destroyed"* (2 Corinthians 4:8-9).

The sufferings of this dark, sinful earth cannot be compared with the eternal glory that will one day be ours.

CHAPTER 10

THREE HOURS
OF DARKNESS

*Now from the sixth hour there was darkness
over all the land unto the ninth hour.*

— MATTHEW 27:45

Have you ever been in such a dark place that you actually thought God had forgotten and forsaken you?

Your so-called friends left long ago, your closest confidants have also departed, telling people they didn't know you, and even some members have said, "I don't want anything to do with him (or her)."

Have you been there? Are you there now? So dark, so lonely, that no one will come to your aid—not even God Himself.

What happens in such a situation? We gather our strength, try to pull ourselves together, and ask the Lord, "My God, why have you forsaken me? Why are you so far from helping me? Can't you hear my cry? Can't you see what's happening? Nobody cares. No one will even try to help me—not even You, God."

Jesus Himself cried these words while hanging on a cross being crucified as the sin-offering for the world.

A MOMENT OF DESTINY

The darkest day had to come. It was set in motion before mankind was created and before a sin was ever committed. The blackest moment in the history of the universe took place—and was so unparalleled it will never need to be repeated.

A sinless Man, the Lord Jesus Christ, was forsaken by the Father, but only in the sense that God allowed Him to die. Jesus, God manifest in the flesh, was physically put to death. *"For he hath made him to be sin for us, who knew no sin; that we might be made the righteousness of God in him"* (2 Corinthians 5:21).

On the cross, *"one of the soldiers with a spear pierced his side"* (John 19:32). This (like so many other aspects of the crucifixion) was in direct fulfillment of Old Testament prophecies. Zechariah wrote, *"...they shall look upon me whom they have pierced"* (Zechariah 12:10).

We know that the Almighty can see, listen, and react

to all things at all times, but in this case, God could hear, but could not answer. On the cross, Jesus was saying, *"My God, my God, why hast thou forsaken me? why art thou so far from helping me, and from the words of my roaring? O my God, I cry in the day time, but thou hearest not; and in the night season, and am not silent"* (Psalm 22:1-2).

"MY GOD"

Judgment for sin—past, present, and future—had to be dealt with by this slain Lamb of God.

During the time Jesus walked on this earth and went about His earthly ministry, He referred to God as *"My Father"* (Matthew 7:27). But while suffering on the cross, Jesus called Him *"My God"* (Mark 15:34)—*"why hast thou forsaken me?"*

Judgment for sin—past, present, and future—had to be dealt with by this slain Lamb of God.

You see, God is so holy, He could not even look on this scene at Calvary, much less hear or answer the plea of Jesus. Why? Because if Christ had been spared, humanity could not have been delivered.

The Great Jehovah came through for Noah and for Abraham, Isaac, and Jacob. But not now—not even for

His own Son.

For His entire life on earth, Jesus took the lowest place among men. He was born in a manger, rejected by His own people, scarred, and spit upon.

Now on Golgotha's hill, they laughed at His plight. His enemies mocked, *"He saved others; himself he cannot save. If he be the King of Israel, let him now come down from the cross, and we will believe him. He trusted in God; let him deliver him now, if he will have him: for he said, I am the Son of God"* (Matthew 27:42-43).

WHERE WERE HIS FRIENDS?

His friends were gone, the disciples had fled, and Christ had no helper, not even His own Father.

Before this day, the relationship between Father and Son had never been broken, but now it would be severed because Jesus was bearing the sin penalty of the world. His friends were gone, the disciples had fled, and Christ had no helper, not even His own Father.

He was surrounded by enemies. David called them the *"bulls of Bashan"* (Psalm 22:12). The word *bull* represents the demon possessed—and these were the people who wanted to see Jesus die.

Even today, your friends and family might leave you,

but your enemies will come around to watch you suffer. They will ask and ask, "Where is God now? I thought you were a Christian. Why can't you get a prayer answered?"

AN ASSEMBLY OF THE WICKED

Crucifixion was the most horrible form of death ever devised by evil men. The Gentiles (Romans) who carried this out against Jesus were there to witness His death. It was an assembly of the wicked—and this includes the scribes, Pharisees, priests, and religious leaders of Israel. They were all present to see the death of "the perfect one," the Messiah, who purposely laid down His life as a sacrifice.

They watched with perverse satisfaction as the soldiers nailed Him to the cross in complete humiliation. He hung there naked as they parted His garment and gambled for the coat (the prayer shawl or tallit) He was wearing. This fact was written about a thousand years before this event (Psalm 22:18; Matthew 27:35).

The Son of God prayed again, *"But be not thou far from me, O Lord: O my strength, haste thee to help me"* (Psalms 22:19).

THE SKIES TURNED BLACK

You may ask, "If God does His best work at night, why was Jesus crucified during the daytime?"

Take a closer look!

The same God who sent His Son to earth has the power to separate darkness from light. At the moment of Christ's death on the cross, the skies suddenly turned black. It was exactly as God inspired the prophet Amos to write: *"And it shall come to pass in that day, saith the Lord GOD, that I will cause the sun to go down at noon, and I will darken the earth in the clear day* (Amos 8:9).

At Calvary, *"from the sixth hour there was darkness over all the land unto the ninth hour [noon until 3 P.M.]"* (Matthew 27:45).

Once more, God was doing His best work!

THE FINAL SACRIFICE

Jesus was placed on the cross at the 9 A.M., *"the third hour"* (Mark 15:25). But we must note the fact that from noon to 3 P.M. (the latter being the hour when Christ died) was the time of the Jewish evening sacrifice. As scripture records, darkness covered the land during that three hour period.

The priest was in the temple getting ready the final

sacrifice of the day. At 3 P.M. they would take the perfect (Pascal) lamb and make it ready to die. You see, if everyone did not come to the temple or bring a sacrifice (perhaps they forgot or were ill), this last lamb was slain for all.

When the priest killed the Pascal lamb and the blood was applied for everyone, he would say with a loud voice, "It is finished"—meaning there was no need for any more sacrifices because the perfect lamb had been placed on the altar for the sins of all the people.

It is significant that at the three o'clock hour, Jesus, the Perfect Lamb of God and the final sacrifice for mankind, looked up to heaven and said, *"It is finished"* (John 19:30).

THREE ETERNITY-CHANGING HOURS

I thank the Lord every day for what He did at Calvary. The cross made it possible for us to have eternal life.

- Three hours of darkness and the price for our salvation was paid in full.

- Three hours of darkness and heaven is ours.

- Three hours of darkness and generation after generation shall be saved.

- Three hours of darkness and the work was finished.

- Three hours of darkness and our souls shall live forever in the Light.

"Who is this King of glory?" (Psalm 24:10). Jesus the Messiah! Jesus the Good Shepherd. Jesus the Savior.

Praise the Lamb of God who came to take away the sins of the world—including yours, including mine!

JESUS – THE LIGHT OF THE WORLD

I am the light of the world: he that followeth me shall not walk in darkness, but shall have the light of life.
– John 8:12

Most of us cannot fathom what it must be like to be totally blind, to be trapped without light, stumbling, hesitant, and dependant as we move around.

In the Bible, darkness often symbolizes sin, but can also refer to not knowing where to go, what to do, or what our purpose is. As the prophet Isaiah wrote, *"We grope for the wall like the blind, and we grope as if we had no eyes: we stumble at noon day as in the night; we are in desolate places as dead men"* (Isaiah 59:10)

In a world without light we are oppressed, our vision is narrow, and our walk is limited. Darkness is our captivity and upsets our very existence. This is exactly what Job experienced during his time of testing: *"A land of darkness, as darkness itself; and of the shadow of death, without any order, and where the light is as darkness"* (Job 10:22).

A life with no direction demonstrates the captivity of living without being able to truly see.

THE LOWEST PIT

Darkness is not only the name of a physical location, it is also a spiritual place. As scripture tells us, *"The people that walked in darkness have seen a great light: they that dwell in the land of the shadow of death, upon them hath the light shined"* (Isaiah 9:2).

In our carnal world, the lack of light often becomes a breeding ground for violence, afflictions, anguish, and confusion. David counseled, *"Have respect unto the covenant: for the dark places of the earth are full of the habitations of cruelty"* (Psalm 74:20).

Psalm 88 was written in remembrance of the descendants of Korah, who rebelled against Moses. It describes a dismal place of imprisonment, with no way out. *"Thou hast laid me in the lowest pit, in darkness, in the deeps. Thy wrath lieth hard upon me, and thou hast afflicted me with all thy waves. Thou hast put away mine acquaintance far from me; thou hast made me an abomination unto them: I am shut up, and I cannot come forth"* (Psalm 88:6-8).

Scripture tells us of many levels of darkness we may

travel through in the process of being set free. But in the final analysis, there is only one source of illumination that can transform a heart and turn night to day. It is Jesus—the Light of the World.

HOPE IN THE DARKNESS

There are countless articles, photos, and paintings portraying Jesus as the Light of the World. One of the most renowned was painted by the English artist William Holman Hunt in 1854. It shows Christ knocking on a door covered with brambles, symbolizing the Lord wanting to enter a sinner's soul (Revelation 3:20). Jesus is holding a lantern, depicting Christ as the Light of the World (John 9:5), providing hope in the darkness.

You must open the door of your heart from the inside, allowing Jesus to enter.

It was while he was painting Jesus that Hunt had a personal revelation of Christ and became a committed believer.

In Hunt's depiction, there is no latch on the door—and this is the way it must be. You must open the door of your heart from the inside, allowing Jesus to enter.

THE GOLDEN LAMPS

Twice in John's gospel we find Jesus making the claim of being the Light of the World.

The first time the Lord made this statement He was in Jerusalem for the Feast of Tabernacles (also called the Feast of Lights). This honored God as He led the Jews from Egypt and through the wilderness desert to the Promised Land.

These lights were so large and had such illumination that they whole city could see them.

On the first day of this feast, two great lanterns (golden lamps) were lit. They stood on each side of the altar. These lights were so large and had such illumination that the whole city could see them. Their brightness beamed all the way across the valley to the top of the Mount of Olives.

Never forget what guided the children of Israel during their forty years in the wilderness. The Lord *"went before them by day in a pillar of a cloud, to lead them the way; and by night in a pillar of fire, to give them light"* (Exodus 13:21).

They were required to stay several thousand feet behind the cloud, and they did not leave the camp when it stopped. But when the cloud moved, they could not linger behind. This cloud was their protection, their sanctuary. The glory of the Lord was in both the cloud and in the pillar of fire.

It was at this Feast of Lights celebration when Jesus proclaimed, *"I am the light of the world: he that followeth me shall not walk in darkness, but shall have the light of life"* (John 8:12).

SIGHT TO THE BLIND

The second time Jesus made this statement was as He was walking in Jerusalem near the temple area and saw a man who was blind from birth.

Nobody paid attention to this poor fellow, and even the disciples asked, *"Master, who did sin, this man, or his parents, that he was born blind?"* (John 9:2).

Jesus answered that neither the man or his parents were at fault. Rather, it was so *"the works of God should be made manifest in him"* (verse 3).

This is also the reply Jesus gave to Mary and Martha when Lazarus died. "Why Lord?" they questioned.

Jesus answered, *"This sickness is not unto death, but for the glory of God, that the Son of God might be glorified thereby"* (John 11:4).

There are many ways the works of God are

manifested—in creation, in salvation, in divine healings, even the raising of the dead.

THE TRUE LIGHT

During the encounter with the man born blind, Jesus said, *"I must work the works of him that sent me, while it is day: the night cometh, when no man can work. As long as I am in the world, I am the light of the world"* (John 9:4-5).

Unless Jesus could back up such a claim He would become a blasphemer, a laughing stock to the scribes and Pharisees.

Please understand that unless Jesus could back up such a claim He would become a blasphemer, a laughing stock to the scribes and Pharisees.

You see, the cloud and the pillar of fire during Moses' day led three million people, but Jesus is now saying that He is the light of the "whole world."

After Jesus uttered these words, He spat on the ground, made some clay, put this mixture on the man's eyes and told him to go wash in the pool of Siloam.

The blind man did as Jesus asked, and came back healed. His sight was completely restored (verse 7).

It is important to note that the Lord asked this man to

do something. This is a pattern we see throughout scripture. For example, Joshua's army had to walk around Jericho seven times before the walls came tumbling down. And after dealing with the woman accused of adultery, He said, *"Neither do I condemn thee: go, and sin no more"* (John 8:11).

THE UPROAR

After Jesus healed the man who was born blind, there were a variety of reactions to the miracle. His neighbors wondered, "Is this the same person?"

They asked him what had happened, and he exclaimed, *"A man that is called Jesus made clay, and anointed mine eyes, and said unto me, Go to the pool of Siloam, and wash: and I went and washed, and I received sight"* (verse 11).

But when they took him to the Pharisees and leaders (priests), it caused a great uproar. They chided, *"This man is not of God, because he keepeth not the sabbath day. Others said, How can a man that is a sinner do such miracles?"* (verse 16).

But the now-healed blind man said Jesus was a prophet.

135

RESTORED VISION

The case became more complicated when the Pharisees spread the word the man was not really blind to begin with. So they found his parents, who responded, "He is of age, ask him."

The Pharisees called him in for questioning the second time. They tried to tell him that Jesus was a sinner, but the former sightless individual made a great statement. "One thing I know, that, whereas I was blind, now I see" (verse 25).

Praise God! He was no longer in darkness.

It is significant to know that the man first referred to the healer as *"Jesus"* (John 9:11), then a *"man...of God"* (verse 33), and finally he calls Him *"Lord"* (verse 38).

His vision restored, he could now see his parents, his neighbors, flowers, trees, rivers, etc. But best of all, he could see Jesus, the Light of the World.

This man is symbolic of each of us. We all are born blind and in darkness. For this reason we need our spiritual eyes to be opened.

The Light of the World comes only to those who will receive Him. Some, like the Pharisees, still deny the Lord. As scripture tells us, *"The light shineth in darkness; and the darkness comprehended it not"* (John 1:5). Jesus was *"in the world, and the world was made by him, and the world knew him not. He came unto his own, and his own received him not"* (verses 10-11).

YOU ARE A LIGHT!

Let me ask, what prison of darkness are you in today? Are you blind to the color of a man's skin? Are you blind because of someone's social standing?

During the Sermon on the Mount, Jesus points His finger at us, saying, *"Ye are the light of the world"* (Matthew 5:14).

What prison of darkness are you in today?

Are you a real follower of Christ, a true believer, a shining light? If so, you are commissioned to have a great influence on the whole world. Jesus declared, *"A city that is set on an hill cannot be hid. Neither do men light a candle, and put it under a bushel, but on a candlestick; and it giveth light unto all that are in the house. Let your light so shine before men, that they may see your good works, and glorify your Father which is in heaven"* (verses 14-16).

Light is made to shine, and the Son of man, Jesus, came to earth to illuminate the Father and glorify God.

Likewise, men, women, and children should be able to see Christ visible in us. Wherever we go we should bring honor to His name. Our business is to shine—and we are called to expel the darkness and bring the brightness of the Lord to mankind.

"NOW I SEE!"

Jesus had compassion on the blind man, but many around him were also sightless—they could not see God's Son, even though He was in their presence.

The meaning of this lesson is clear. The light is for *all*. May God help us to have a personal encounter with Jesus that is so life-changing that we too can rejoice and shout, "I was blind, but now I see!"

Look around. The world is filled with darkness, sorrow, and death. The responsibility rests upon you and me to be "sons of the light," to illuminate the Son of God who can bring blinded souls out of the darkness.

The world is watching and waiting.

NO MORE NIGHT!

God is saving His best for last.

Very soon, the Almighty is going to give the signal for Gabriel to blow his trumpet—and it will happen in the midnight hour. Scripture clearly tells us that *"the day of the Lord so cometh as a thief in the night"* (1 Thessalonians 5:2).

What a moment that will be!

And where we are headed is beyond description. Since there will be no more work for our heavenly Father do to, He is going to eliminate night completely.

Here is how heaven was revealed to John: *"And the city had no need of the sun, neither of the moon, to shine in it: for the glory of God did lighten it, and the Lamb is the light thereof. And the nations of them which are saved shall walk in the light of it...And the gates of it shall not be shut at all by day: for there shall be no night there"* (Revelation 21: 23-25).

Because you have received God's best—His only begotten Son, the Light of the World—your darkness is about to end forever!

NOTES

_____

_____

_____

_____

_____

_____

_____

_____

_____

_____

_____

_____

_____

_____

_____

_____

_____

_____

FOR BOOKS AND MEDIA RESOURCES
OR TO SCHEDULE THE AUTHOR FOR SPEAKING
ENGAGEMENTS, CONTACT:

TOMMY COMBS
HEALING WORD
LIVING WORD MINISTRIES
P.O. BOX 1000
DORA, AL 35062

PHONE: 1-866-391WORD (9673)
INTERNET: www.tommycombs.org
EMAIL: tommy@tommycombs.org